IMAGES
of America

THE TEXAS
RANGERS

IMAGES
of America

THE TEXAS RANGERS

Chuck Parsons

ARCADIA
PUBLISHING

Published by Arcadia Publishing
Charleston, South Carolina

Printed in the United States of America

Library of Congress Control Number: 2010940824

For all general information, please contact Arcadia Publishing:
Telephone 843-853-2070
Fax 843-853-0044
E-mail sales@arcadiapublishing.com
For customer service and orders:
Toll-Free 1-888-313-2665

Visit us on the Internet at www.arcadiapublishing.com

To Bill and Karon O'Neal and Bob Alexander and
Jan Devereaux, four dear friends who have traveled
many, many miles of the Old West with me

CONTENTS

ACKNOWLEDGMENTS

To Bob Alexander, Maypearl, Texas; John M. Baker, Lockhart, Texas; Cheryl Beesinger, librarian of the Archer City Public Library, Archer City, Texas; Donaly E. Brice, Lockhart, Texas; Leonard A. Bucsanyi, Kerrville, Texas; Joe B. Davis, Kerrville, Texas; Jean Eckstein, Kerrville, Texas; Peggy Engledow, Prairie Lea, Texas; Gary P. Fitterer, Kirkland, Washington; Dale Fry, Llano, Texas; Jody Edward Ginn, Austin, Texas; Erin Hall, Kerrville, Texas; Stephen L. Hardin, Abilene, Texas; Kurt House, San Antonio, Texas; H. Joaquin Jackson, Alpine, Texas; Byron A. Johnson, director of the Texas Ranger Hall of Fame and Museum, Waco, Texas; Jack Loftin, Windthorst, Texas; Ray Martinez, New Braunfels, Texas; David A. Smith, Houston, Texas; Sharon E. Spinks, New Braunfels, Texas; Christina Stopka, Waco, Texas; and to my Arcadia editors Lauren Hummer, Kristie Kelly, and Emma Parker, thank you!

FOREWORD

The Texas Rangers have been serving the people of Texas and protecting its borders for over 185 years. Their history began when Stephen F. Austin, known as the "Father of Texas," saw a great need to protect the early settlers from the Indians who claimed this land as their own. He learned what Spain and Mexico already knew: they could not rid this territory of the Indians.

The Comanches, known as the Lords of the Plains, proved to be the fiercest fighters. They were the first Indians to use the horse and, when mounted, had a great advantage over their enemies. Their primary weapons were the bow and arrow and the lance. At close range, their arrows proved a highly effective weapon. In 1823, Austin realized the dangers that the Indians presented and hired 10 men to act as Rangers. They were to scout the areas near the settlements and warn the settlers when Indians were in the vicinity. It was from this beginning that the Texas Rangers, in time, would become a household name across Texas. They were the gallant men who rode the range, protecting their homes and engaging their attackers in battle against all odds.

The Rangers were officially organized in 1835 when the interim Texas government approved and established a corps of Texas Rangers. It authorized three companies of 56 men, each headed by a captain and aided by a first and second lieutenant. Robert M. Williamson was elected major, and he would direct the operations of the companies. The first three elected captains were Isaac Burton, William Arrington, and John J. Tumlinson. Privates who signed on for one full year of service were paid $1.25 per day. Each Ranger had to furnish his own arms, ammunition, and mounts. This included a good horse and 100 rounds of powder and ball.

When the Texas war for independence broke out, the Rangers fought Mexicans as well as Indians. During the siege of the Alamo, the only reinforcements to come to the aid of Travis were members of a mounted Ranger company from Gonzales led by Capt. George Kimbell. They shared the same fate as the Alamo defenders and became known as the Immortal Thirty-Two.

Sam Houston ordered the Rangers to act as a fighting rear guard to his army and to observe enemy troop movements. After the victory at San Jacinto, the Republic of Texas still needed Rangers. More settlers started arriving in Texas and continued to migrate west. Texas had no money and only a small army that was too expensive to arm and deploy. The Rangers served as an inexpensive paramilitary force, made more affordable because they furnished their own arms and mounts. In short, the Texas republic needed the Rangers. It was during this time that names such as John Coffee "Jack" Hays, Samuel H. Walker, Ben McCulloch, and "Big Foot" Wallace began appearing on the Ranger muster rolls. These men took on the Comanches, defeating them in various battles such as Plum Creek and Walker Creek. It was in the latter engagement that Hays first used the five-shot Colt Paterson revolver.

In 1845, Texas became a state. Shortly thereafter, the war with Mexico began. The US Army was commanded by Gen. Zachary Scott. Scott called on Jack Hays to command the 1st Regiment of Mounted Volunteers. These men were to act as scouts, as they were familiar with the territory that was to be invaded. Rangers such as Big Foot Wallace, Sam Walker, Ben McCulloch, Ad

Gillespie, and John Ford served well. Their exploits during the Mexican War brought the Rangers national attention.

It was during this time that Sam Walker, on a recruiting mission, met Sam Colt. Walker told Colt about his experience fighting the Indians and how the Colt Paterson revolver made a difference but needed improvement. Together, Walker and Colt designed a more powerful revolver in .44 caliber with a cylinder holding six shots. It weighed over four pounds and could easily be reloaded while on horseback. These became known as Walker Colts. The collaboration between Walker and Colt saved Colt from bankruptcy. The Colt Manufacturing Company was established because a Texas Ranger helped design the most powerful weapon needed at the time.

During the decade following the Mexican War, the Rangers primarily acted as volunteer companies, raised when the need arose and disbanded when their work was done. One of the best-known Rangers of this era was John S. "Rip" Ford, a medical doctor, lawyer, newspaper editor, and former mayor of two cities. When the outlaw Juan Cortina took over the border city of Brownsville in 1859, the Texas government dispatched Ford and a company of Rangers to take care of the bandit. Cortina was defeated in a running gun battle with the Rangers. Many of Cortina's men were killed, as were some Rangers. Ford later wrote that "his company of brave men knew their duty and they did it. They did right because it was right."

During the Civil War, with most of the young men off fighting on eastern battlefields, a regiment of Rangers stayed behind to protect frontier settlements. After the war and during Reconstruction, law enforcement was handled by an organization known as the Texas State Police, which was disbanded in 1873. In 1874, after Reconstruction, Texas elected a new governor, Richard Coke. Texas still had an "Indian problem," but it also had a lawlessness problem. Outlaws such as Sam Bass, Bill Longley, and John Wesley Hardin became notorious. The legislature created two Ranger forces: the Frontier Battalion commanded by Maj. John B. Jones and a Special Force captained by Leander H. McNelly. In a short period, the Frontier Battalion had drastically reduced the "Indian problem" and began to concentrate on restoring law and order. Numerous fugitives from justice were captured or killed during this period. Texas's deadliest outlaw, John Wesley Hardin, was captured in Florida by Rangers John B. Armstrong and John R. Duncan, with the assistance of Florida lawman William Henry Hutchinson. McNelly and his men worked on the Rio Grande frontier and reduced banditry. The Texas Rangers now became a significant law enforcement body. They worked to establish order, tracking outlaws, preventing riots, quieting feuds, and suppressing crime and discord throughout the state.

By 1900, the Frontier Battalion and Special Force had reduced crime so much that the legislature reduced the force and passed a new law. This law authorized four Ranger companies with a maximum of 20 men per company, each company serving under a captain who would select his own men. The men still had to furnish their own horses, weapons, and attire, and they had no standard badge.

During the first two decades of the 20th century, while still dealing with the usual drifters and desperadoes, the Rangers found themselves confronted with problems as new as the century itself. In 1910, the Mexican Revolution began, and the violence in Mexico spread across the Rio Grande. On several occasions, Mexican bandits raided into Texas. The Rangers were sent to the border with orders to keep raiding parties out of Texas and to make the raiders understand that if they did cross the river they would be doing so at the peril of their lives. In 1918, the national Prohibition law was passed, giving the Rangers yet another problem to cope with along the border. Many a burro train of bootleg whiskey from Mexico was intercepted, and shootouts between Rangers and smugglers were not infrequent.

As Texas changed, so did the Rangers. Among those who made the transition from horseback to automobile was Frank Hamer. Hamer was involved in many shootouts along the border and then became senior captain in 1922. Later, he was instrumental in tracking down the notorious killers Bonnie Parker and Clyde Barrow.

In 1934, the Texas Senate formed a committee to investigate crime in law enforcement. This group produced a report that was highly critical of law enforcement but proposed a solution: the creation of the Texas Department of Public Safety, today known as DPS. A bill was introduced to create this agency, which would operate under a three-member public safety commission. The Rangers would be transferred from the adjutant general's office, and the highway patrol would be moved from the highway department to form this single state agency. The Rangers would consist of 36 men. With the creation of the DPS, the Rangers would have professionalism to match their tradition. They had the benefits of a state-of-the-art crime laboratory, improved communications, and better training. Their duties would be the same as they had been for years—to enforce the laws of the state. The Rangers were now the criminal investigation branch of the DPS. They wore no uniform but dressed in true Texas style with boots and Stetsons.

Today, the Texas Rangers still investigate major crimes and protect the borders along the Rio Grande. They have increased their size to 144 commissioned officers and are divided into seven companies that are scattered throughout the state. Each company is headed by a captain. The Rangers are stationed in various towns throughout each company's assigned area. From horseback to high tech, the modern Rangers are better trained, better equipped, and with state-of-the-art investigative tools, they continue to protect the people of Texas. They proudly wear the Cinco Peso (five cent) Badge, originally cut from a Mexican coin, and continue to preserve the traditions in a new era. As Col. Homer Garrison Jr., former director of the DPS and chief of the Texas Rangers once said, "As long as there is a Texas there will be the Texas Rangers."

I am a fifth-generation Texan and a descendant of George Lamb, who fought at the Battle of San Jacinto. He was a flag bearer and one of the first to be killed. Lamb County in North Texas is named for him. This is one reason why I have always had a great interest in Texas history. When I was growing up in Texas in the 1940s and 1950s, I was fascinated with great Western heroes such as Roy Rogers, Gene Autry, and Hopalong Cassidy. They wore white hats, and thanks to them, good always won over evil. One of my favorites was the Lone Ranger. It was during this time that I became acquainted with the real Texas Rangers. I learned of their service to the citizens of the state. I learned that the "Ranger" was real, and that was what I wanted to be like. *Tales of the Texas Rangers* was one of my favorite radio programs. Joel McCrae played the Ranger, and the stories were based on real crimes. It later became a television series, and the technical advisor was a former Ranger named "Lone Wolf" Gonzaullas. When I was 14 years old, I wrote to Colonel Garrison and asked him if he could send me information on the Rangers and a Ranger badge to add to my collection. A few weeks later, I received a letter from Colonel Garrison stating that I would be receiving the old-style Ranger badge he had authorized Simmangs Badge Company in San Antonio to make for me. He also sent me a pamphlet from the DPS about the Texas Rangers.

I wrote to Colonel Garrison again when I turned 21 and told him I still had a great interest in the Texas Rangers and wanted to know how I might become one. He sent me an application to join the DPS and told me that the Rangers were chosen from the DPS and that I needed at least five years of experience as a police officer before I could apply. I filled out the application form, and after going through a background investigation and interview, I was accepted into the DPS Academy in Austin in February 1963. The school started with 68 recruits, and when the class graduated in June, only 28 men were left.

Upon graduation, I became a highway patrolman, first stationed in Houston and then in Katy, Texas. In 1968, I applied for a position with the DPS Intelligence Service. After going through the interview process, I got one of the vacancies and was promoted to agent. I knew the job would get me into the criminal-investigation section of the DPS and might help me down the road to become a Texas Ranger. In 1969, the state legislature authorized 10 new positions in the Texas Rangers, which raised the number from 62 to 72.

To make a long story short, I applied for the job I had always wanted. I drove to Austin and met with Chief Jim Ray, who at the time was the head of the Criminal Law Enforcement Division. During the interview, I showed Chief Ray the badge Colonel Garrison had sent me and let him know that I wanted a real one. A couple of months later, Chief Ray called and told me I was going to get one of the vacancies. I was only 28 years old and had reached my boyhood dream. My station would be in Company F at Austin and my captain would be Clint Peoples, my promotion effective as of October 1, 1969. During my Ranger career, I worked on a lot of major cases involving murders, armed robberies, rapes, burglaries, cattle thefts, and vice crimes including gambling and prostitution. I was furnished all the equipment necessary to solve a crime, including a fingerprint kit, camera, and investigation crime kit. I was furnished an unmarked car, a .357 revolver, riot shotgun, and a high-powered rifle. I was constantly going to various criminal investigation schools and firearms training classes. I was being prepared for any type of situation that I might face as a Ranger, from a riot to a prison break.

During my Ranger career, several of my investigations drew statewide publicity. One of the most rewarding cases I worked was when I solved the burglary of the house of Col. Homer Garrison. He was deceased at the time and a lot of his guns and badges had been taken. I was always thankful to Colonel Garrison for helping me to get the direction I needed to become a Texas Ranger.

I was stationed in Austin until 1980, when I requested to transfer to Kerrville in the Texas Hill Country after a vacancy became available. It's the ideal station for a Texas Ranger and a great place to raise a family. I was a Texas Ranger for 24 years, retiring in 1993. I never regretted my decision to be a Ranger and wear the coveted Cinco Peso Badge. It's not easy being a Ranger, as the people you serve expect you to solve whatever crime has been committed. You have a great tradition to uphold, and when your time is up you want to turn it over to the next Ranger in as good shape as you received it.

—Joe B. Davis

One

RANGER ORIGINS

Although everyone knows something about the Texas Rangers, the oldest state-level law enforcement body in the United States, few know the details of their origins. Historians accept 1823 as the advent of the Rangers. On January 7, 1823, John F. Tumlinson Sr. and Robert H. Kuykendall Sr. wrote a letter to Jose Felix Trespalacios, the Mexican governor of Tejas, requesting permission to form a company of men to protect settlements on the lower Colorado and Brazos Rivers.

On May 5, 1823, *empresario* (entrepreneur) Stephen F. Austin mustered Lt. Moses Morrison and a company of nine volunteers into service to protect the settlements of what is now Texas but was then part of Mexico. US Army veteran Morrison organized the company and marched to a creek near the mouth of the Colorado River, their intention to build blockhouses for frontier protection. However, due to the inadequacy of building materials and their own limited powder and ball, they failed in their mission, exerting most of their energies merely to survive.

At this time, the tribes resisting the increasing number of white invaders were the Comanches, the Kiowas, the Apaches, the Karankawas, the Wacos, and the Caddos. Within a few decades, only the Comanches and the Kiowas were left, the others having been essentially wiped out or forced to relocate.

To combat the tribes, the Mexican government encouraged white settlers to move into the 15,000-square-mile colony along the Colorado, Brazos, San Jacinto, and San Bernard Rivers. In spite of no known mineral deposits such as gold or silver, American settlers wanted land for farms and ranches. It was an opportunity for a new life for themselves and their families. At this time, the Tejanos (Texans of mixed Spanish or Mexican and Indian ancestry) welcomed the newcomers, as they provided additional protection against marauding Indian parties. The seat of the Mexican government was 1,000 miles away. There would be no cavalry from the south or from the east to protect them. From the beginning, the Rangers answered the call.

No photograph of Stephen Fuller Austin—the "Founder of Anglo-American Texas"— exists, but he did pose for at least two miniature paintings that showed the sculptor of this statue how Austin looked. This likeness marks his grave in the Texas State Cemetery. Austin's contribution to Texas history is virtually immeasurable. The group of nine volunteers he mustered under the command of Lt. Moses Morrison was the beginning of the Texas Rangers. John J. Tumlinson Sr. and Robert H. Kuykendall Sr. saw the need to form a militia company for the protection of settlers coming into the frontier. This land became the 28th state in the union, the Lone Star State. (Author's collection.)

One of the bloodiest battles between Rangers and Indians occurred on November 10, 1837, in what is now Archer County. Lt. A.B. Von Benthuysen and 15 Rangers were following a trail of stolen horses when they met a party of Kichais and Cherokees. One Ranger perceived that an Indian was intending to shoot him and quickly fired, killing the Indian. Almost 150 Indians attacked the Rangers near what is known as the Stone Houses. The Rangers fought for nearly 90 minutes, losing four men, before the Indians set fire to the grass and attempted to surround the surviving Rangers. Von Benthuysen led his men through the smoke but lost six more Rangers. The survivors managed to escape on foot. The historical marker was erected in 1970. (Both, Jack O. Loftin.)

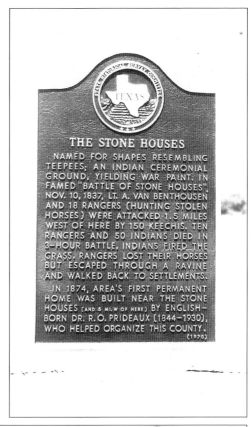

Alabama native Creed Taylor came with his family to Texas in 1824. Among the first significant events of his life was to help defend the Gonzales "Come and Take It" cannon. He participated in various battles against the Mexicans in the Texas Revolution. Following the Alamo's fall, he led his family to safety during the Runaway Scrape, then fought in the Battle of San Jacinto. He also fought at the Battle of Plum Creek in 1840, joining Capt. Jack Hays to fight the Indians. He saw further action during the Mexican War as a private in Capt. Sam Walker's Texas Mounted Rangers. During the post–Civil War period, members of his extended family were deeply involved in the Sutton-Taylor feud. Taylor's dictated memoirs in the book *Tall Men with Long Rifles* were published by James T. DeShields in 1935. Taylor died December 26, 1906, and is buried in Kimble County. In 1936, the Texas Centennial Commission erected a monument to DeWitt County pioneers. Creed Taylor's name appears on it twice, as a soldier in the Texas Revolution and as a participant in the Battle of Salado in 1842. (Robert G. McCubbin Collection.)

Four historians are pictured at the site of the Creed Taylor home in Kimble County. Taylor's house, built in 1869, was considered the finest home west of San Antonio. This historical marker points out that Creed Taylor joined the Rangers and served in various battles—at Bandera Pass and at Salado—and served in the Mexican War. Shown here, from left to right, are Peter R. Rose, Chuck Parsons, Frederica Wyatt, and Donaly E. Brice. (Author's collection.)

For many Texas Rangers, documentation to prove service remains sparse. Shown here is a rare certificate showing Creed Taylor's service in the mounted volunteers from September 28 through November 8, 1835, signed by Robert M. Coleman. Much valuable documentation was lost when the capitol burned to the ground in 1853. (Texas State Archives.)

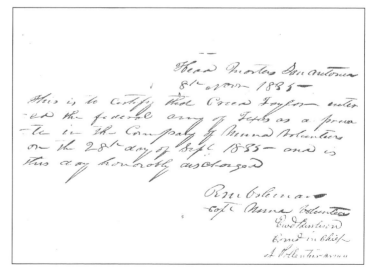

This engraving was not intended to be an accurate portrayal of an early Texas Ranger, but it does exemplify the concept of rough men being armed to the teeth. It first appeared in the popular national publication *Harper's Weekly* in 1861. Historian Stephen Hardin described it as "a paradigm of mythical Texas Ranger images." Note the lasso, revolvers, knife, ax or tomahawk, and rifle. (Author's collection.)

Benjamin McCulloch failed to reach the Alamo due to a case of the measles. However, he joined Houston's army as it retreated eastward and then commanded one of the "Twin Sisters" cannons at San Jacinto. He earned a reputation as an Indian fighter while serving under Capt. Jack Hays. McCulloch also served during the Mexican War and was later killed during the Civil War at the Battle of Pea Ridge on March 7, 1862. He is buried in the Texas State Cemetery. (Author's collection.)

These three unidentified Comanche warriors appear as did most who participated in fighting white settlers and Rangers. Texans fought Comanches, known as the "Lords of the Plains," until the Indians were decisively defeated in 1874 at the Battle of Palo Duro Canyon. The finest horsemen of the Great Plains were beaten due to the numerical superiority and better weapons of the Anglos. (Author's collection.)

Henry McCulloch, brother of Ben, joined the Texas Rangers as a citizen-soldier. He fought in the Battle of Plum Creek in 1840 and later fought in the Battle of Salado Creek. McCulloch was elected sheriff of Gonzales County in 1843. During his fighting career, he rose to the rank of brigadier general. McCulloch is buried in the Geronimo Cemetery in Seguin. (Western History Collections.)

This image of Comanche warriors most likely was made during the latter half of the 19th century, although the typical warrior changed little in appearance through the centuries. The warriors who raided the coastal city of Linnville and then Victoria prior to the Battle of Plum Creek could have appeared very much like these men. Of all the threats to settlers on the Texas frontier, the Comanches were the most feared. (Author's collection.)

One of the most notable battles between white settlers and Rangers against the Comanches began in August 1840 near Plum Creek in present-day Caldwell County. This 1978 painting by Lee Herring depicts the battle. After a terrifying raid by the Comanches on two communities in South Texas—Linnville and Victoria—settlers gathered and attacked on the Comanches' return north. The settlers inflicted heavy casualties and forced the Comanches to give up their vast amount of plunder. (Caldwell County Genealogical and Historical Society.)

This historical marker commemorating the Battle of Plum Creek is in the Lions Club City Park in Lockhart, the county seat of Caldwell. The 600 Comanche and Kiowa warriors, with many of their women and children, were attacked by approximately 200 Texans. The war party stretched for miles across the prairie, hence there is no one particular "site" of the battle. This costly defeat resulted in the Comanches raiding farther west. (Author's collection.)

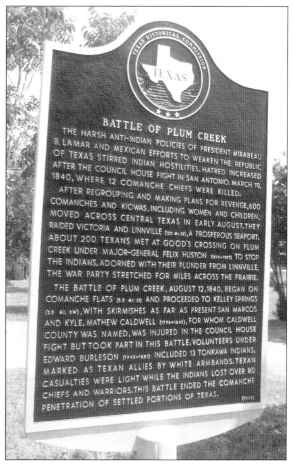

GEN. EDWARD BURLESON.

North Carolina native Ed Burleson served in the War of 1812 and spent much of his life in some aspect of military service. Burleson arrived in Texas in 1830, and due to increasing attacks on settlements was commissioned in June 1836 to form ranging companies to patrol between the Colorado and Brazos Rivers. Burleson found success in fighting Indians and Mexicans (he was at San Jacinto) but not in the political arena, as he lost to Anson Jones in his bid for president of Texas. Burleson died December 26, 1851, and is buried in the Texas State Cemetery. (*The Indian Wars and Pioneers of Texas.*)

The names of Andrew Jackson Sowell, father and son, loom large in Texas history. The father was an Alamo defender and courier and was sent out to obtain needed supplies. Before he could return, the Alamo had fallen. He fought in the Mexican War and continued fighting in America's Civil War. A.J. Sowell Sr. died in 1883. His son, shown here in an image made about 1871 when he was 23 years old, joined the Rangers and fought against Indians in the campaigns of 1870 and 1871. He later wrote several books about early Texas history, and although some of the facts are questionable, they are nevertheless of great value to historians. Among them are *Rangers and Pioneers of Texas* (1884), *Early Settlers and Indian Fighters of Southwest Texas* (1890), and *Life of Big Foot Wallace* (1899). (Western History Collections.)

John Coffee "Jack" Hays remains one of the best known of the early Texas Rangers. His fighting in the Battle of Plum Creek ensured his renown; the Comanches christened him "Devil Jack." A Mexican War veteran, he later served as sheriff of San Patricio County, California, and was named surveyor-general of that state. He laid out the city of Oakland, California. (Western History Collections.)

The most famous encounter between Jack Hays and Indians is a myth in spite of two historical markers designating its occurrence and describing the engagement, one erected in 1936 and the other in 1965. Near Llano is the Enchanted Rock marker erected in 1936 stating, "From its summit, in the fall of 1841, Captain John C. Hays, while surrounded by Comanche Indians who cut him off from his ranging company, repulsed the whole band and inflicted upon them such heavy losses that they fled." (Pat Parsons.)

NINE MILES WEST
IS THE
ENCHANTED ROCK

FROM ITS SUMMIT, IN THE FALL OF 1841
CAPTAIN JOHN C. HAYS
WHILE SURROUNDED BY COMANCHE
INDIANS WHO CUT HIM OFF FROM HIS
RANGING COMPANY, REPULSED THE
WHOLE BAND AND INFLICTED UPON THEM
SUCH HEAVY LOSS THAT THEY FLED

Erected by the State of Texas
1936

Jack Hays made such an impression on Texans that Hays County was named after him. On the northeast corner of the courthouse square in San Marcos is this impressive, larger-than-life equestrian statue of Hays. Actually, Hays lived many more years in California than he did in Texas. (Bill O'Neal Collection.)

The three historians standing on the mythical Enchanted Rock in 1992 are, from left to right, Gary P. Fitterer, Barry A. Crouch, and Donaly E. Brice. Today, the rock rests in the 1,643-acre Enchanted Rock State Natural Area and is situated on the Gillespie-Llano county line. The legend of Jack Hays fighting off the Comanches is only one of the tales involving the fascinating boulders that are popular among the thousands of tourists who visit annually. Again, there is no solid evidence that Jack Hays ever engaged the Comanches from the peak of Enchanted Rock. (Gary P. Fitterer.)

Quanah Parker (shown here with two of his wives) and Kicking Bird (below) were two Comanche warriors who, during the 1860s and early 1870s, resisted the onslaught of white settlers. Kicking Bird, also known as Humming Bird, after spending his youth combating white settlers, chose to try the white man's way of life by 1873. Many of his tribe opposed him. He was poisoned in May 1875, presumably by the Comanche who disapproved of his new philosophy. The son of a white captive and a Comanche warrior, Parker became the most feared of Comanche fighters. After his defeat at the Battle of Palo Duro Canyon in 1874, however, he was forced to surrender. He managed to live peaceably in the white man's world and died a natural death in 1911. (Both, University of Texas at El Paso, Special Collections Department.)

Samuel Colt is best remembered for his invention of the revolver. In reality, Colt only perfected the concept of the revolving cylinder in the pistol; there had been efforts to make a successful revolver prior to Colt's attempt. He patented his version in England in 1835 and in the United States in 1836. Until that time, the Comanches—described by historian Joseph G. Rosa as "the finest light cavalry in the world"—had the advantage. With only a single-shot weapon, Texans were at a great disadvantage, but with Colt's pistol holding six shots, Texans finally had the upper hand. After improvements to his initial attempts, Colt eventually found complete success. His name became synonymous with the revolver that "won the West." Colt is pictured with one of his pistols that "made [every man] equal." (Both, Western History Collections.)

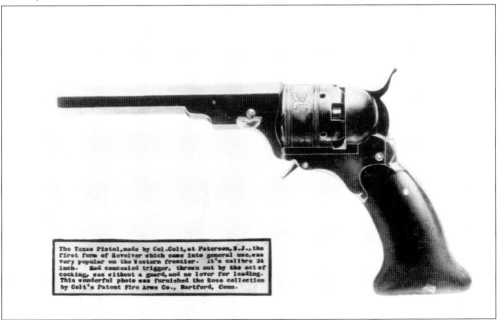

The Texas Pistol, made by Col. Colt, at Paterson, N.J., the first form of Revolver which came into general use, was very popular on the Western frontier. It's calibre 34 inch. Had concealed trigger, thrown out by the act of cocking, was without a guard, and no lever for loading. This wonderful photo was furnished the Rose collection by Colt's Patent Fire Arms Co., Hartford, Conn.

Gen. John R. Baylor (left), brother of the better-known George W. Baylor, is shown with William Alexander Anderson Wallace in this photograph by N. Winther taken some time during the 1870s. Wallace was known as "Big Foot" Wallace due to his size-12 foot. Kentucky native Baylor arrived in Texas in 1840 and soon joined John H. Moore's ranging company intending to fight Indians. He narrowly escaped death at the Dawson Massacre and then managed to survive the Confederates' dismal attempt to conquer the New Mexico Territory during the Civil War. He was named provisional governor of Arizona during the Civil War. Wallace joined the Rangers and for a time fought Indians and Mexicans, then found a more peaceful pursuit in driving a stagecoach between San Antonio and El Paso. He became a folk hero and at his death on January 7, 1899, was buried in the Texas State Cemetery. (Western History Collections.)

Two

CONFLICT INCREASES

Mexico encouraged white settlers to move into Texas, the best-known group being Stephen F. Austin's "Old Three Hundred." This was a group of families gathered together by Austin for establishing homes and colonies on the Brazos River in present-day Washington County and south into what is now Colorado County. Mexico's law required settlers to be Catholics and to have no trading with "foreign states," which meant Louisiana as well as the United States and Europe. The religious requirement and the trade laws were basically ignored.

The term Rangers referred to men willing to operate independently from a regular military organization, providing their own weapons and horses and other necessities. Capt. Moses Morrison's first Ranger group consisted of nine men: Cpl. John McCrosky and Pvts. Caleb R. Bostwick, Pumpry Burnitt, John Frazer, William Kingston, Aaron Linville, Jesse Robinson, Samuel Sims, and John Smith. These early Rangers experienced considerable combat with warlike tribes. Capt. Abner Kuykendall fought the Karankawas in June 1823; John J. Tumlinson Jr. and his men engaged Waco near present day Columbus. Tumlinson also routed a Waco war party in what is now Fayette County during the winter of 1828–1829.

By April 1825, empresario Green DeWitt had established a colony. Its capital was Gonzales. This community experienced frequent scenes of violence and terror over the next few decades. Near Gonzales on April 15, 1836, a total of 13 traders were slaughtered by a much larger group of Comanches. Bartlett D. McClure, later immortalized in the novel and motion picture *True Women*, followed the Comanches and exacted vengeance. Among his men were Mathew Caldwell, later a famous Ranger captain, William S. Foster, a future Secretary of War, and Almaron Dickinson, who in less than a year would perish defending the Alamo.

Events spiraled toward increasing violence in Mexico City as Santa Anna rose to power and became a dictator. As tension increased between Tejas and Mexico City, conflict with Indians also increased. Men such as John H. Moore, Robert M. Coleman, Phillip H. Coe Sr., and Robert M. "Three-legged Willie" Williamson gained considerable renown. On December 10, 1836, Coleman's Ranger company was the first formally constituted by Texas law.

During the years of Indian-Texan warfare, a white family's greatest fear was losing the children to raiders. Of those children abducted, few were ever reunited with their families. Brothers Jefferson D. and Clinton L. Smith, sons of former Ranger Henry M. Smith, were taken on February 26, 1871. Three years later, they were ransomed, but by this time they were more accustomed to the Indians' manner of living. Herman Lehmann was abducted May 16, 1870, and through the years virtually "became" an Indian. During his years as a captive, he actually fought Texas Rangers on one occasion. Shown in this picture are, from left to right, Jeff Smith, Clinton Smith, Texas Gov. Dan Moody, Herman Lehmann, and William B. Krempkau, a noted trail driver. The woman standing behind the Smiths is unidentified. This image was made at a rodeo at Comfort on August 18, 1929. Note the bow in Lehmann's hands. J. Marvin Hunter recorded the memoirs of the Smith brothers in a book entitled *The Boy Captives*, first published in 1927. (Western History Collections.)

Capt. Cicero R. Perry of Company D, Frontier Battalion, doubtless had good reason to use a cane after having been severely wounded any number of times in engagements with Mexicans and Indians. Although he was a good tracker, even the best occasionally had reason to depend on another man's skills. Perry (holding the cane) is shown in 1874 with the mysterious Brazlinscom, who by reputation was among the best in tracking war parties. (Western History Collections.)

Perry's prowess as a fighting man may have been learned from John Coffee "Jack" Hays, shown here in a portrait that seems to attest to his fighting abilities. Hays took superior weapons into every fight and used them with skill. Hays remains an iconic Texas figure. He was called "Devil Jack" by the Comanches and created enough enmity with the Mexicans to have a $500 bounty placed on his head. He later created a legacy in California. (Western History Collections.)

C.R. Perry died October 7, 1898, and is buried in Johnson City in Blanco County. He served with distinction in numerous engagements with Indians and in the Mexican War. He pursued deserters, draft dodgers, and outlaws during the Civil War years, and was the first captain of Company D of the Frontier Battalion in 1874. He recorded the memoirs of his Indian fighting days and of life on the frontier. (Author's collection.)

Henry Mims, a lucky survivor of being scalped by Indians, claimed to be a Ranger, although no official record of his service has been located. Wounded, scalped, and left for dead in 1869, he survived and lived to be 109 years old. He died in Globe, Arizona, in 1925. Rangers also occasionally scalped their victims. (Western History Collections.)

Many men who were Rangers later served as county sheriffs. James Francis Blair was in the Mexican War and the Civil War, rising to the rank of captain of Company G of the 36th Texas Cavalry. On June 25, 1866, during the days of the Sutton-Taylor feud, Gov. James W. Throckmorton appointed him sheriff of DeWitt County. He served until February 15, 1869. The state historical association set this marker above his grave in 1969. (John M. Baker.)

Tennessee-born Joseph Tumlinson was brought to Texas when Stephen F. Austin began territorial colonization. After Indians killed his father, Tumlinson joined the avenging party to track down and kill those responsible. On September 28, 1835, he joined Robert M. Coleman's Rangers and served in other companies as well. Following the Civil War, Tumlinson served for 10 months in Gov. E.J. Davis's state police who were stationed in DeWitt County. During Reconstruction, he was considered a leader among the followers of William Sutton in their feud with the Taylors. After surviving a lifetime of violence, he died peacefully in bed on November 25, 1874. (Samuel H. Tumlinson Collection.)

When the Civil War ended, "Captain Joe," as Tumlinson was popularly called, served in the unpopular Texas State Police organization created by Governor Davis in an unsuccessful effort to reduce the amount of violence in the state. He survived much violence during his adult years. Tumlinson is buried in the family cemetery, but his grave has been neglected. (Author's collection.)

Ideally, the paper trail following the Rangers of the 19th century would be complete. For Joseph Tumlinson, at least one document did survive. Shown is a paymaster's certificate of pre–Civil War service. This certifies that Tumlinson served as a guide in his father's company of mounted volunteers from April 1 to June 16, 1860. (Author's collection.)

Three

A COMANCHE DEFEAT AND FAMILY FEUDS

Amidst conflict, the nascent Texas government planned for the uncertain future and created ranging districts. On November 9 and 24, 1835, the government wrote two articles specifying the creation of a force known as the Corps of Rangers, the first time the word Ranger appeared in legislative documentation.

The Corps of Rangers consisted of 56 men in a company, each company commanded by a captain and two lieutenants. Each man was to provide his own horse, arms, and rations. The immediate commander was Robert M. "Three-legged Willie" Williamson; the other captains were John J. Tumlinson Jr., William H. Arrington, and Isaac W. Burton.

On March 2, 1836, the Texas Convention appointed Sam Houston as general in chief of all Texas regulars, volunteers, and Rangers. Numerous battles took place between the rebelling Texans and Mexicans as conflict between the Texans and Indians continued. The siege and fall of the Alamo has become known worldwide. Among its defenders were George C. Kimbell and his Gonzales Ranging Company and 20 other men of Gonzales, known collectively as the Immortal Thirty-Two.

During the next few decades, conflict continued between the three groups—Indians, Texans, and Mexicans. Anglo "cowboys" ranged into Mexico to steal livestock, and banditti from south of the Rio Grande raided into the Nueces Strip, the land between the Nueces River and the Rio Grande, to plunder. At the same time, Comanches and other tribes still sent out marauding parties. Much of the state was a virtual no-man's-land.

One of the most notorious raids was committed by a large Comanche war party plundering and destroying the town of Linnville and raiding Victoria. Rangers and settlers attacked the raiders near Plum Creek in present-day Caldwell County. The citizen soldiers gave the Comanches a devastating defeat on August 12, 1840. This engagement is known as the Battle of Plum Creek. Among the combatants were several who have become famous in Texas Ranger history: John Coffee "Jack" Hays, Edward Burleson, John Henry Brown, Mathew Caldwell, Benjamin McCulloch, Henry McCulloch, Alexander Roberts, and Creed Taylor.

Serving six years as a Texas Ranger in the 1870s, James Buchanan Gillett survived fighting outlaws and Indians. "Jim" Gillett guarded John Wesley Hardin after his 1877 capture, assisted in the apprehension of the Horrells, arrested Eli Wixon without firing a shot, and later became city marshal of wild El Paso City. Born in 1856, Gillett lived well into the 20th century, dying on June 11, 1937. His book remains a classic of Ranger writing. He is buried in the Marfa Cemetery. This photograph, taken in 1879, is important as it shows Gillett with the tools of the trade—horse (Dusty), Winchester, pistol, and knife. According to Gillett, the "original picture was taken on tin-type, which made it appear backwards." The image is reversed here to show the gun and pistol on his right side, as he actually wore them. (Western History Collections.)

Highly educated George B. Erath hailed from Vienna, Austria, but in 1833 made Texas his home and began his career as a surveyor. He joined John H. Moore's Rangers and fought Indian raiders. He fought in the Texas Revolution and was at the Battle of San Jacinto. Following those exciting years as a Ranger, Erath entered the political arena representing Milam County and was later elected to the First Legislature. Erath's legislative work allowed Gov. H.R. Runnels to authorize the creation of a company of 100 Rangers under Capt. John S. Ford. Erath died May 13, 1891, and is buried in Oakwood Cemetery in Waco. This statue of Erath stands in front of the Texas Ranger Hall of Fame. (Pat Parsons.)

Capt. Daniel Webster Roberts (left) lived an adventurous life and left an account of his days as a Ranger, as did his wife, Lou. In later years, Roberts frequently visited with his former comrades. He is shown with John O. Biggs, who participated in the Deer Creek fight with Roberts in 1873. Biggs was never a Ranger, but Roberts began his Ranger career in 1874. (Western History Collections.)

Daniel Roberts, captain of Company D, was rare in that he was allowed to have his bride share Ranger camp life with him for six years. They both wrote their reminiscences in later years. Roberts—who lived from October 10, 1841, to February 6, 1935—and his wife—who lived from September 14, 1867, to July 14, 1940—lie together for eternity in the Texas State Cemetery beneath modest stones. (Pat Parsons.)

Many families provided Rangers for the state—as well as men willing to fight and die in a family feud—and none was more famous than Creed Taylor. After youthful adventures against Mexicans and Indians, he left his ranching interests in central Texas and located in the Texas Hill Country. There he built a substantial home. This image shows the Taylor home with Creed standing on the lower floor, his white beard plainly visible. (Western History Collections.)

The original two-story home of rancher Creed Taylor was built in 1869 and was considered the finest residence west of San Antonio. It burned in 1926. Rebuilt by Dillard Stapp, it again burned in 1956. Creed Taylor had left the turbulence of his home country to find peace in Kimble County, where this marker stands today. (Author's collection.)

Elmer Kelton grew up on a ranch in West Texas. Never a Ranger nor even a successful cattleman, Kelton became a word master and produced numerous wonderful books about Texas and the Texas Rangers. His trilogy, *Ranger's Law*, *Texas Vendetta*, and *Jericho's Road* were later republished under the title *Ranger's Law*. His novels earned him seven Spur awards from the Western Writers of America as well as numerous other awards. (Bill O'Neal Collection.)

Some Rangers were conscious of the history they created. Thomas P. Gillespie stayed in touch with his Ranger companions for years. In 1928, at a Ranger reunion, he was photographed with other Rangers, possibly by Noah H. Rose. Seen in this photograph are, from left to right, (seated) Capt. Dan W. Roberts and Gillespie; (standing) Ed Conn, W.W. Lewis, James Bomar, Henry Wishworth, and Will Traweek. (Western History Collections.)

A group of old-time Rangers gathers in Menard County. During the 1870s, battles occurred with Indians as well as white outlaws. It was only natural that the old-timers would gather in a central location such as Menard, the county seat. Some are identified here. Included in this picture are (first row) Maj. William M. Green (far left in dark hat), president of the Ex-Rangers Association; (second row) William Jennings Hale (fourth from left), and Jim Bomar (13th from left); (third row) Captain Roberts (far left), his wife Lou Roberts (second from left), and William W. Lewis (third from left). (Robert E. Hale Sr.)

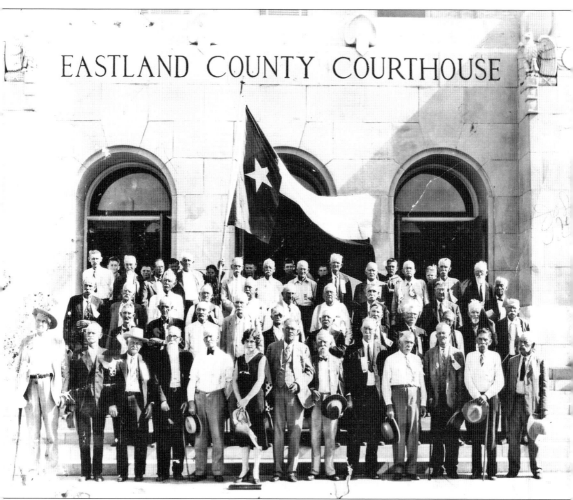

William M. Green organized the Texas Ex-Rangers Association. He had joined Capt. John R. Waller's Company A in 1874, and the first assignment was to break up the John Wesley Hardin gang in Comanche County. This they did, although numerous men were lynched instead of standing trial. During the 1920s, the ex-Rangers met in various towns in the Hill Country. This image dates from 1930 when the group met there on August 30. They discussed the old days when they were satisfied with their $40-per-month salary and plenty of adventure. In this image are Ruby Mae Green, secretary-treasurer of the organization (sixth from the left in the first row); and to her immediate left is her father, Major Green. Major Green died on December 23, 1930, in Colorado City. (Author's collection.)

Texas had plenty of family feuds from the earliest days of the frontier to the early 20th century. Usually, the Rangers were called in to stop the feuding violence. Among the bloodiest and longest was the Sutton-Taylor feud of central Texas, which covered numerous counties. The sons and nephews of Creed Taylor were participants, as was Creed's brother Pitkin. Sons Hays and Doboy were killed, as was Pitkin. Creed escaped the feud by locating in Kimble County. (Donald F. Frazier.)

John Wesley Hardin killed many men in Texas, all justified in his mind as self-defense or because he was in a kill-or-be-killed situation. After participating in the Sutton-Taylor feud, Hardin fled the state and hid out for three years in Florida, where Texas Rangers John B. Armstrong and John R. "Jack" Duncan captured him. (Robert G. McCubbin Collection.)

Four

THE FRONTIER BATTALION

In 1845, Gen. Zachary Taylor arrived in Texas to acquire the land from Mexico either by negotiation or by military conquest. The area at stake was present-day Texas, New Mexico, Arizona, California, and parts of Utah, Colorado, and Nevada. Taylor mustered several companies of Rangers. Men such as Jack Hays, George T. Wood, and Ben McCulloch became famous. Rangers were considered brutal fighters by their enemies and were christened by Mexicans Los Diablos Tejanos—the Texas Devils. Rangers were with General Taylor in taking Monterrey, Mexico, and with Gen. Winfield Scott in capturing Mexico City. At war's end, the Rangers were mustered out at Veracruz.

But conflict between the two countries continued. From Mexico, Gen. Juan Cortina increased raiding on Texas soil. In one battle, Cortina defeated a troop of Rangers led by Capt. W.G. Tobin. A retaliatory raid led by Col. John S. Ford in 1859 defeated Cortina in a battle in Mexico.

With the Civil War in the eastern states a reality in 1861, Gov. Sam Houston saw most Rangers marching off to fight on eastern battlefields. To provide some protection on the frontier, the Frontier Regiment was created as well as the Texas Mounted Rifles and the Border Regiment. By the grace of location, Texas was spared from destructive battles, but by the end of the war there was economic, social, and political turmoil. Texas now faced Reconstruction.

To create a semblance of stability, Gov. E.J. Davis created a state militia and a state police force. These frontier forces were Rangers in fact if not in name. Adjutant General James Davidson deployed Ranger forces under John W. Sansom and Henry J. Richarz to West Texas to combat Kickapoo and Lipan Apache. Cesario Falcon and Bland Chamberlain were sent to South Texas to reduce banditry.

Although conflict would continue with Indian raids and Anglo and Mexican outlawry, a new era was on the horizon with the election of 1873. Governor Davis was voted out, Richard Coke was voted in, and the glory years of the Texas Rangers were ahead.

Aten Family "1886" Round Rock, Texas

The Aten brothers made themselves famous in Ranger history. This family photograph shows them before their Ranger years. Pictured from left to right are (first row) Calvin Grant, Rev. Austin Aten, and Catherine E. and Edwin Dunlap; (second row) Ira D., Clara B., Thomas, Angie, and Frank Aten. Ira, Cal, and Ed all became Rangers and served in Company D of the Frontier Battalion. They were in numerous gunfights, but none was ever wounded. (Former Texas Rangers Association.)

Ira Aten left the Rangers on the insistence of his bride-to-be, Imogene Boyce. On February 3, 1892, he and Imogene were married in Austin. He later accepted the position of sheriff of Castro County. In spite of her earlier dire threats, Imogene Aten now became the jailer. The Atens later left these employments to someone else and moved to California, where they spent the rest of their lives. (Former Texas Ranger Association.)

Wedding picture of Ranger Ira Aten & Imogene Boyce. Feb. 3, 1892

Both Thomas P. Gillespie (seated) and James B. Gillett enlisted into Company E on September 1, 1877. Gillespie had served under Lt. Daniel W. Roberts. He served under Lt. N.O. Reynolds until April 30, 1879, and then ranched in Tom Green County. Gillespie died June 11, 1926, at the age of 72. He is buried in Fairmount Cemetery in San Angelo. (Author's collection.)

James Buchanan Gillett appears more as a dude in this rare photograph, possibly a wedding portrait. After his six years with the Rangers, he resigned in December 1881 and served as assistant city marshal of El Paso. He then became city marshal in June 1882. Gillett married Helen Baylor, daughter of Ranger Capt. George W. Baylor, but the marriage ended in divorce. On May 1, 1889, he married Lou Chastain in San Marcos. Gillett's *Six Years with the Texas Rangers* describes his career. (Archives of the Big Bend.)

Leander H. McNelly died from tuberculosis on September 4, 1877. In honor of his memory and to recognize what McNelly had done to recover stolen cattle from his massive King Ranch, Capt. Richard King purchased this $3,000 monument and erected it on his grave at Burton, Washington County. This image shows the storm-damaged obelisk, since repaired. (Author's collection.)

Capt. L.H. McNelly, during his pursuit of absconding Adjutant General James Davidson in 1873, stopped in Montreal, Canada, for this now-famous photograph made by James Inglis. Davidson fled the state with public funds but found sanctuary in New Zealand, where he spent the remainder of his life. (Texas Ranger Hall of Fame and Museum.)

In the early 1930s, Dr. Walter Prescott Webb persuaded William Crump Callicott to record his, Callicott's, memoirs for Webb's book, *The Texas Rangers: A Century of Frontier Defense*. Though nearly blind at the time, Callicott carefully described what it was like to serve as a Texas Ranger under Captain McNelly. Due to his failing eyesight, Callicott could only write when the sun was bright, and so wrote on the porch of his home. Callicott is shown here after his Ranger years, living in Houston. He left a valuable record of his days as a Ranger. He served first under Capt. John R. Waller in Company A, then joined McNelly's militia unit of Rangers, enlisting on April 1, 1875, and serving until February 15, 1876. (David A. Smith.)

Pictured are three Rangers of the 1870s. This image was in Gillett's personal collection, but there is no positive information as to the identification of those shown. The dark-skinned man seated to the left is most likely William Scott Cooley. Capt. Cicero R. Perry swore him in as a sergeant in Company D on May 25, 1874 . It was said that Cooley was part Indian, but in spite of his dark appearance, this is not correct. Nor did Indians kill his parents, as some have written. He did, however, harbor a bitter hatred for Indians. After his friend Tim Williamson was murdered by a mob, Cooley resigned his Ranger position and took up the vengeance trail. After several killings, he succumbed to death, perhaps from "brain fever," as some have written, but most likely as the result of his whiskey being poisoned by an unknown hand also looking for revenge. Cooley died June 10, 1876. (Author's collection.)

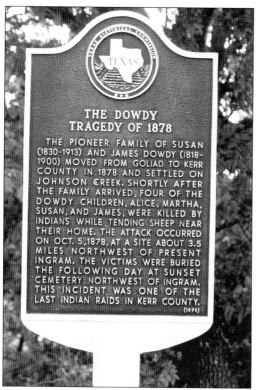

THE DOWDY
TRAGEDY OF 1878

THE PIONEER FAMILY OF SUSAN
(1830-1913) AND JAMES DOWDY (1818-
1900) MOVED FROM GOLIAD TO KERR
COUNTY IN 1878 AND SETTLED ON
JOHNSON CREEK. SHORTLY AFTER
THE FAMILY ARRIVED, FOUR OF THE
DOWDY CHILDREN, ALICE, MARTHA,
SUSAN, AND JAMES, WERE KILLED BY
INDIANS WHILE TENDING SHEEP NEAR
THEIR HOME. THE ATTACK OCCURRED
ON OCT. 5, 1878, AT A SITE ABOUT 3.5
MILES NORTHWEST OF PRESENT
INGRAM. THE VICTIMS WERE BURIED
THE FOLLOWING DAY AT SUNSET
CEMETERY, NORTHWEST OF INGRAM.
THIS INCIDENT WAS ONE OF THE
LAST INDIAN RAIDS IN KERR COUNTY.
(1979)

The Frontier Battalion's original mission in 1874 was to reduce the Indian raids in the western settlements. By 1878, this mission was essentially accomplished, but on October fifth, raiders attacked the Dowdy ranch and killed four children who were tending their flock of sheep. This marker was erected in 1979 to commemorate the family tragedy. Rangers under Lieutenant Reynolds were sent to pursue the raiders but never caught them. (Author's collection.)

The Dowdy family plot is located in the Sunset Cemetery northwest of Ingram. Four of the family children—Alice, Martha, Susan, and James Dowdy—were tending the family's sheep when attacked by Indians, with Mexicans and white outlaws possibly mixed in as well. Their bodies were gathered up and buried the following day in these shell-covered graves. Some vandalism has occurred to the stones since this image was made. (Author's collection.)

Prior to moving to Texas, Nelson O. Reynolds served in the last days of the Civil War. He joined Company D of the Frontier Battalion under Capt. C.R. Perry in May 1874. By September 1877, he was lieutenant commander of Company E. In his later years, Reynolds settled in Center Point, Kerr County. Members of the Reynolds family are buried in the Center Point Cemetery. (Author's collection.)

During the frontier years, William Steele was adjutant general. He was the man between the governor and Maj. John B. Jones, head of the Ranger companies in the field. Steele graduated from West Point in 1840, fought Indians, and served in the Mexican and Civil Wars. He was boss of the Rangers from January 1874 until January 1879. (Author's collection.)

James B. Hawkins, a Ranger in the 1870s, found obeying orders from Company D commander Capt. Frank M. Moore difficult. He was dishonorably discharged on November 5, 1876, for "mutinous and insubordinate conduct." Shown in this 1875 tintype, he displays his weapons: a Winchester, a Colt six-shooter, and a Bowie knife. There was no uniform, nor was a badge necessary. (Author's collection.)

Years after his Ranger service, James B. Hawkins served as Custer County, Montana, sheriff. Even as an elderly gentleman, Hawkins, shown here as sheriff, had not lost the fire that had caused his discharge from the Texas Rangers. He had also worked as a buffalo hunter in Montana, using the powerful Sharps rifle as a normal tool of the trade. (Custer County Museum.)

James W. Guynn began as a lieutenant when joining Capt. Leander H. McNelly's Ranger company. Guynn also contributed various newsy letters to the hometown newspaper, the *Colorado Citizen*. Later, he was accidentally shot while deer hunting and died July 2, 1882. He is buried in the Odd Fellows Rest Cemetery in Columbus. (Author's collection.)

Shown is James William Guynn's final resting place in a Columbus cemetery. The original stone placed by the family merely provided his name and the dates of his earthly existence. His veteran's marker reveals that he served as a first lieutenant of the 24th Regiment Texas Cavalry. It fails to mention he was a McNelly Ranger from June 22 to August 31, 1875. (Author's collection.)

Lee Hall came to Texas in 1869. In August 1876, he was commissioned as second lieutenant under Captain McNelly. As McNelly's replacement, Hall reduced the violence of the Sutton-Taylor feud in South Texas. After resigning in 1880, he managed the Dull Brothers Ranch. He died on March 12, 1911, and is buried in the national cemetery in San Antonio. (Author's collection.)

Missouri native Cornelius Vernon "Neal" Coldwell was the first captain of Company F of the Frontier Battalion. His most notable Ranger work was during the "Kimble County Roundup" in April 1877. He was later captain of Company A and on May 9, 1879, was named Frontier Battalion quartermaster. Coldwell died on November 1, 1925. (Western History Collections.)

CAPT NEAL COLDWELL

John B. Jones, born in South Carolina on December 22, 1834, was chosen head of the Frontier Battalion in 1874. He told his men to be ever alert and always ready for action. Jones took command on May 2, 1874, and immediately selected the captains of the six companies. He dealt with marauding Indians, family feuds, racial hatreds, and Anglo outlaws as well as the necessary paperwork required to administer an organization containing hundreds of men. Jones's college training helped him deal with the paperwork, but his war experience as a member of the 15th Texas Infantry helped him deal with the fighting men. In 1879, he was appointed adjutant general. Jones died July 19, 1881, and is buried in Oakwood Cemetery in Austin. His impressive monument is shown here. (Right, Western History Collections; below, author's collection.)

Frank M. Moore, a native of Weakley County, Tennessee, served as captain of Company D of the Frontier Battalion. In Texas history, he is better known as sheriff of Kerr County during the wild frontier days. Elected November 7, 1882, Moore was reelected into office and resigned on November 8, 1892. During the Civil War, he served in Company B of the 36th Texas Cavalry. Once having chosen Kerr County of the Hill Country as his home, Moore remained there the rest of his life. Shown are his impressive headstone and bronze military marker. He is one of the 32 Texas Rangers buried in the Center Point Cemetery. (Left, Bob Alexander Collection; below, author's collection.)

Bear Creek served as a camp for Rangers during the 1870s and into the 1880s. The historical marker near Junction, Kimble County, was erected in 1966. Lt. Nelson O. Reynolds established this camp during his months scouting for renegade Indians and white outlaws who roamed the banks of the Llano River and its tributaries. (Author's collection.)

In contrast to the beauty of Reynolds's Bear Creek camp, Capt. George W. Arrington's territory was almost desolate in appearance, judging from this photograph of a white-shirted Arrington standing center before his 20 men of Company C. The individuals in this photograph have frequently been identified as Capt. Jack Hays and his men, but that is erroneous. (Western History Collections.)

George Washington Arrington was born John C. Orrick Jr. To avoid prosecution for alleged acts during Reconstruction, he chose his mother's maiden name and became a different man. Arrington is best remembered as the captain of Company C of the Frontier Battalion. He joined the Rangers on August 31, 1874, serving honorably under B.S. Foster, J.M. Denton, and Neal Coldwell before being named as captain of Company C on May 1, 1879. He resigned on August 31, 1882. On November 7, 1882, he was elected sheriff of Wheeler County and served until November 4, 1890. Later, he was appointed sheriff of Hemphill County, serving from November 30, 1894, until November 3, 1896. Arrington died on March 31, 1923, and is buried in the Old Mobeetie Cemetery in Wheeler County. (Western History Collections.)

George P. Durham served under Captains McNelly and Hall in the dangerous bandit-infested area known as the Nueces Strip. He joined McNelly in 1875 and served through 1877. Durham then married Caroline Chamberlain and spent the remainder of his life working on the huge King Ranch. His memoir, *Taming the Nueces Strip,* was published in 1962. (Western History Collections.)

Thomas L. Oglesby entered the Special Force as a private on January 11, 1878. He served under Neal Coldwell, Guy B. Broadwater, and J.L. Hall before being named captain on March 1, 1881. Oglesby resigned from the service on November 25, 1882. He was elected sheriff of Maverick County on November 7, 1882, reelected in 1884 and 1886, and served until November 8, 1892. (Author's collection.)

Patrick "Pat" Dolan served the law both as a Texas Ranger and a county sheriff. Named first as captain of Company F, he later served as captain of Company A. Dolan worked the Kimble County Roundup of outlaws in April 1877 and was elected on November 6, 1888, as sheriff of Jeff Davis County. He served until November 4, 1890. (Western History Collections.)

Edward A. Sieker was one of four brothers who served in Company D of the Frontier Battalion, joining on May 25, 1874. He served honorably under Captains Perry, Moore, and Roberts, and resigned on August 31, 1880. Sieker died on April 17, 1901, and is buried in the Pioneer Rest Cemetery in Menard. (Western History Collections.)

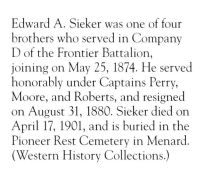

No one served longer in the Frontier Battalion than Ranger Lamartine Pemberton Sieker, shown here in his Civil War uniform. Born April 8, 1848, he served in the Confederate army from 1863 to 1865, and by 1873 he was in Texas. He joined Company D of the Frontier Battalion, commanded by Capt. C.R. Perry, on May 25, 1874. On September 1, 1882, Sieker was named captain of Company D. From 1901 through 1905 he served as quartermaster. Sieker died in Houston on November 13, 1914, and was initially buried there, but his remains were later moved to the Texas State Cemetery in Austin. (Western History Collections.)

Vernon Coke Wilson began his Ranger career on September 23, 1876, and served under Neal Coldwell and then under Guy B. Broadwater and Nelson O. Reynolds. Later, he worked for the railroad, investigating robberies. During such an investigation in California, he and deputy Andrew W. McGinnis were shot and killed on September 13, 1892, by robbery suspects Chris Evans and John Sontag. (Western History Collections.)

Richard Ware was the first sheriff of Mitchell County. He was elected on January 10, 1881, and served until November 8, 1892. Ware then became US marshal of the western district of Texas. Some historians claim Richard Clayton Ware shot outlaw Sam Bass at Round Rock, ending the bandit's career. Others, including some of the Rangers who were there, claim George Herold deserves that honor. (Author's collection.)

Richard Clayton Ware was the son of Benjamin F. Ware and was born in Rome, Georgia, on November 11, 1851. By 1870, he was in Texas. He served in Company E under various Ranger captains—first, Lt. Berch S. Foster, then Lt. Nelson O. Reynolds and Lt. Charles L. Nevill. These commanding officers were given the lower-paying rank of lieutenant to save money. Ware later served under Capt. Ira Long and Capt. Bryan Marsh. According to Ranger historian Robert W. Stephens, "As a twenty-seven-year-old Texas Ranger in Company E," Ware "gained distinction by being credited with killing Sam Bass at Round Rock in 1878." This was never proven, however, as others who were there credited George Herold. Ware died on June 25, 1902, and is buried in Colorado City beside his brother Charles Ware, also a former Ranger, and other members of his family. The historical marker was erected by the State of Texas in 1967. (Both, author's collection.)

Shown are two Rangers of the Frontier Battalion in 1877, Charles L. Nevill (standing) and Chris R. Connor. Connor joined Company A on July 11, 1876, but transferred to Lt. N.O. Reynolds's Company E on August 31, 1877, resigning on November 30, 1879. Connor died January 23, 1916. C.L. Nevill joined the Rangers in 1874 and served under various commanders until he was named captain of Company E in 1881. On November 7, 1882, he was elected sheriff of Presidio County and served in that capacity until November 6, 1888. Nevill then moved to San Antonio, where he held various public offices. At his death on June 14, 1906, he was district clerk of Bexar County. His grave is shown in San Antonio City Cemetery No. 6. (Both, author's collection.)

Charles L. and Robert L. Nevill are another example of brothers serving as Rangers. On May 25, 1874, at the age of 19, Charles joined Company D, commanded by Capt. C.R. Perry. He also served under Capt. J.M. Denton and Capt. Neal Coldwell until discharged on December 15, 1876. He joined Lt. N.O. Reynolds's Company E on September 1, 1877, and assumed command on September 1, 1879. He was promoted to captain in 1881. (Author's collection.)

Robert Lafayette Nevill joined brother Charles's command on June 12, 1880, and served until March 28, 1883. He is shown here with his wife, Kate Griffin Nevill, and their two daughters, Kate Mildred (left) and Mary. Robert Nevill never received the attention his brother did. Both Nevill brothers deserve a good biography by a Ranger historian. (Author's collection.)

Nelson O. Reynolds resigned from the Ranger service and was replaced by Charles L. Nevill. Reynolds's resignation letter is dated February 29, 1879. He gave two explanations for leaving: citing health reasons and his dissatisfaction with the recruits who wanted to become Rangers. He recommended Charles Nevill to replace him as commander of Company E, and his recommendation was followed. Reynolds married Irene Temperance Nevill, Charles's sister, on September 13, 1882. This c. 1882 image of Reynolds (left) and Nevill, both in the prime of life, was made by an Austin photographer. Shown below is Reynolds in his twilight years, seemingly at peace with the world. The house still stands in Center Point, Kerr County. (Both, Stephen Reynolds Davis.)

The Sam Bass Gang robbed stagecoaches in the Dakota Territory, held up trains, and planned a bank robbery before they met their downfall at Round Rock in July 1878. Shown is the gang, from left to right: Sam Bass, Joe Collins, John E. Gardner, and Joel Collins playfully and recklessly pointing his cocked pistol at his brother's head. This is the only authenticated photograph of Bass and was probably made in Dallas in 1876. Bass and the Collins brothers died violently; all shot down either during the commission of a crime or in its immediate aftermath. Gardner left the criminal life and lived long, dying on April 23, 1926, at the age of 81. Gardner claimed to have been a Texas Ranger but no record has been located to substantiate his claim. (Western History Collections.)

Notorious outlaw Sam Bass successfully held up trains in North Texas, but his plan to rob the bank at Round Rock led to his death. He became a popular folk hero, and tourists broke off chips of his headstone as souvenirs. Shown in a 1927 photograph are the graves of gang members Seaborn Barnes (left) and Bass. (Western History Collections.)

The Barnes and Bass headstones as they appear today in the Round Rock Cemetery are shown. In the July 19, 1878, gunfight, Barnes was killed outright, Bass died a few days later, and Frank Jackson got away and disappeared from history. Captured by Reynolds's Rangers, Bass died on July 21. Gang member Jim Murphy escaped but died not long afterward in 1879. (Author's collection.)

This image remains controversial, as writers occasionally claim it is Sam Bass and his gang. According to these writers, Bass is the seated figure with pistol in hand, traitor Jim Murphy is on the left holding handcuffs, and Seaborn Barnes is the large figure at right. The seated figure with pistol is actually Thomas O. Bailes, a Ranger of Company E in 1884 and later in Company B. He also was assistant chief of the Capital Detective Association in the 1880s. The young man on the left has been identified as Vernon Coke Wilson, and the man on the right is G.G. Walker, although the identification of both of the men standing is questioned. (Author's collection.)

John Riley (right) and younger brother William L. Banister pose for this tintype at 19 and 17 years old, respectively. As cowboys, they rode the cattle trails north to Kansas. Both enlisted in Lt. N.O. Reynolds's Company E, Frontier Battalion—John on October 9, 1877, and Will on November 20, 1877. Will resigned on November 30, 1880, and married Virginia R. Daniels. He died on January 4, 1921, and is buried in the city cemetery at San Saba. John R. Banister remained in Company E until February 29, 1880. Later, he was elected sheriff of Coleman County and then reelected but died in office on August 2, 1918. His widow completed his term and resigned on November 5, 1918. She was the first woman in Texas, and possibly in the United States, to serve as a county sheriff. (Author's collection.)

No photograph of Charles M. Webb is known to exist, but his name recognition is great as he was a victim of gunfighter John Wesley Hardin in Comanche County on May 26, 1874. Webb had served under J.C. Connell in the Brown and San Saba County Rangers from January 6 to March 26, 1874. His grave in the Greenleaf Cemetery in Brownwood is shown. (Author's collection.)

Hardin was the most wanted man in Texas. This image of him was made in 1875 while he was a fugitive in Florida. Hardin claimed to have killed somewhere around 40 men—all in self-defense, of course. Captured by Rangers and other lawmen in 1877, he was safely returned to Texas to stand trial and was sentenced to a term of 25 years in the Texas State Prison. (Robert G. McCubbin Collection.)

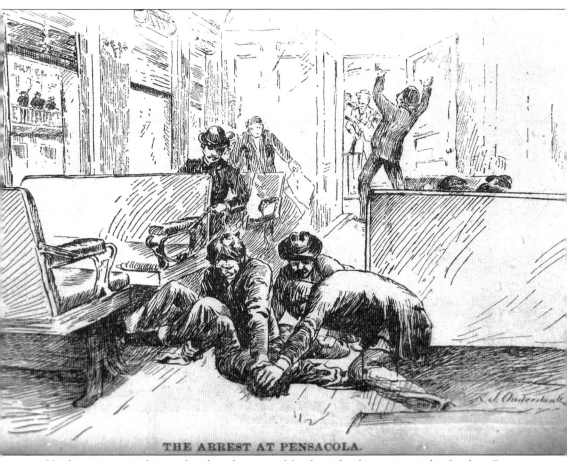

THE ARREST AT PENSACOLA.

Hardin was surprised in a railroad smoker car and fought violently to maintain his freedom. Rangers John B. Armstrong and John R. "Jack" Duncan, along with Florida lawmen Sheriff William H. Hutchinson and William D. Chipley, managed to forcibly corral him. Armstrong finally knocked Hardin out to compel his surrender. In 1895, Hardin's autobiography was published by a printing firm in Seguin and contains several illustrations by Texas artist Robert J. Onderdonk. This is how Onderdonk visualized the capture. One of Hardin's companions, James Mann, was killed in the capture when he foolishly drew a revolver and shot at Ranger Armstrong. (Author's collection.)

These two images of John B. Armstrong show him as a young Texas Ranger. The first shows him as he appeared in the early 1870s, possibly around the time he first joined the Texas Rangers to work under Captain McNelly. The second shows him a few years later, although the exact years of these pictures cannot be determined. Unfortunately, even with numerous images of Armstrong, none show him as many would like to see him—armed, six-shooters pushed forward for show, and a Winchester held in his hands. Nor did he and Ranger Duncan stop along the route to Texas from Florida to have their photograph made, as did the lawmen who captured another noted Texas killer, William P. Longley. (Both, author's collection.)

This is perhaps the most frequently published image of John B. Armstrong, showing him in his later years. Armstrong served in the Rangers from 1875 to 1879 and then chose the more peaceful lifestyle of ranching in south Texas. Following his marriage, he located in what is today Willacy County. Besides his ranching interests, Armstrong drilled for water and worked to bring the railroad to south Texas. He captured Hardin, fought bandits in south Texas, was at Round Rock when the Bass Gang was shot to pieces, and helped capture King Fisher and members of his gang. Armstrong obtained clear title to 50,000 acres of contested ranchland that is now a successful operation still owned and operated by the Armstrong family. Armstrong's grave marker, below, is in the Oakwood Cemetery in Austin. (Both, author's collection.)

In capturing the most wanted fugitive in Texas, John Wesley Hardin, John B. Armstrong, and John R. Duncan did not act alone. Florida sheriff William H. Hutchinson played a vital role by first entering the smoking car and causing Hardin to relax his guard. Hutchinson lived out his life peacefully in Pensacola, Florida. (Author's collection.)

William D. Chipley of the railroad also acted in the capture. This heroic act brought no notoriety to Chipley, and he made no effort to bring attention to himself, probably believing it was part of his job. But he did bring down a man-killer who had become notorious in Texas. (Author's collection.)

The Banister brothers ran away from home in 1867 and settled in Texas. As cowboys they drove cattle up the trail to Kansas. John, pictured here, served in Company E from October 9, 1877, to February 29, 1880. He then worked for the railroad, the Cattle Raisers Association, and was then elected sheriff of Coleman County. There is a state historical marker on his grave in the Santa Anna Cemetery. (Author's collection.)

William and John Banister left home because they wanted adventure in Texas. Will, pictured here, enlisted at Bear Creek on November 20, 1877, serving under Lt. N.O. Reynolds and then under Capt. Ira Long. He resigned from the service on November 30, 1880, and then ranched in the Panhandle. He lost everything during a severe winter. Will died on January 4, 1921, having survived his wife for eight years. He is buried in San Saba, Texas. (Author's collection.)

Thomas H. Mead appears ready to take on anyone brave enough to challenge him. The tall, dark, and handsome Ranger is dressed appropriately in functional clothing, bandana, gloves, knee-high boots, and gun belt with ammunition for both a Winchester and a long-barreled pistol. His Bowie knife appears in front of his holstered pistol. Mead left Texas, and, according to J.B. Gillett, disappeared from history. (Author's collection.)

COL GEO W. BAYLOR.

George W. Baylor first fought Indians and then served under Gen. A.S. Johnston during the Civil War. As captain of Company C, Frontier Battalion, he fought the Apache, campaigning against the dreaded Mimbres Apache chief Victorio in 1879 and 1880. Baylor resigned in 1885 and was elected to the Texas House of Representatives from El Paso. (Western History Collections.)

Among the nearly 1,500 graves in the Center Point Cemetery in Texas are those of 32 Texas Rangers. There may be others whose gravestones have been lost. Each Ranger's grave is now marked with a Texas Ranger memorial cross. The Rangers listed on this marker are W.D.C. Burney, Neal Coldwell, J.A. Gibbens, H.T. Hill, F.L. Holloway, R.J. Irving Sr., R.J. Lange, J.H. Lane, S.T. Lane Jr., T. Lane, M.A. Lowrance, J.L. McElroy, S.G. McElroy, A.S. Moore, Frank M. Moore, G.K. Moore, G.R. Moore, G.W. Moore, H.C. Moore, James Moore, J.T. Moore, M.F. Moore, D.C. Nowlin, J.C. Nowlin, R.W. Nowlin, P. Alonzo Rees, N.O. Reynolds, W.H. Rishworth, J.L. Sellers, A.J. Sowell, W.H. Witt, and S.G. Wray. The headstones of N.O. Reynolds and his wife, Irene T. Nevill Reynolds, are shown here prior to the installation of the Ranger cross. (Both, author's collection.)

Georgia natives Linton Lafayette (right) and Lawrence Baker Wright (below) both served with Captain McNelly in the Sutton-Taylor feud and on the Rio Grande frontier. During the 1875 Palo Alto Prairie fight near Brownsville, a bandit who had lost his horse mounted behind another rider. L.B. Wright saw the pair and fired once; his lucky shot ended the life of both bandits. L.L. Wright served under Duval County sheriff Eugene A. Glover and then became sheriff of Duval County, serving from November 2, 1880, until his defeat 10 years later on November 4, 1890. Brother L.B. later studied medicine in Nashville, Tennessee. He returned to Texas and practiced in Duval County. Both brothers died in February 1892 during an epidemic. (Both, author's collection.)

Arkansas native James Maddox Bell joined Company D Frontier Battalion under Capt. John R. Hughes on September 14, 1894. As a new recruit during this period, Bell would have had to swear an oath stating that he had "not fought a duel with deadly weapons." Bell never gained fame for his services to the state, but he did serve well. Bell died of tuberculosis on July 29, 1897 at age 32. (Western History Collections.)

James Bell, Texas Ranger, Company "D" * 1895.

Mervyn B. Davis experienced adventure as a Ranger under Lt. N.O. Reynolds. One important task he performed was guarding John Wesley Hardin during his murder trial and appeal. Davis observed that Hardin slept more peacefully than some of Davis's fellow Rangers. Later, Davis found a successful career in the newspaper business and was instrumental in bringing a state chapter of the National Audubon Society to Texas. (Carol Davis Wiener.)

Mervyn B. Davis served in the Army of Northern Virginia during the Civil War but by 1873 worked for the *Daily Reporter* in Waco. From September 1877 to March 1878, he was in Company E under Lt. N.O. Reynolds. While serving, he wrote letters about his experiences as a Ranger that were printed in the Dallas newspapers and in the *Galveston Daily News*. He contributed significantly to the National Audubon Society and the Texas Humane Society. After his death on June 18, 1912, his grave remained unmarked. Shown is the military marker that was installed at a special program on May 21, 2005, in Waco's Oakwood Cemetery. Also shown is the marker's unveiling by Civil War historian John A. Stovall and Byron A. Johnson, director of the Texas Ranger Hall of Fame and Museum. (Both, author's collection.)

A.M. "Gus" Gildea, a native Texan, became a wanted fugitive during the turbulence known as the Lincoln County War of New Mexico Territory. In spite of his youthful transgressions, he became a lawman, serving as a deputy sheriff in Tom Green County. He later became a deputy marshal for the western district of Texas. Gildea served in Company D from June 1, 1887, to November 30, 1890. He later worked as a Special Ranger without pay. His later years were filled with pain caused by wounds received during his youth. He died in Pearce, Arizona, on August 10, 1935. This beautiful image shows him as a young man prior to joining the Rangers. (Author's collection.)

Captain D. W. Roberts' Quarters. Captain Roberts and Sergeant L. P. Seiker, standing by the ambulance. Photo by Ragsdale, 1878.

Photographers' names are often lost to history, but McArthur Cullen Ragsdale's is not, thanks to these photographs of Capt. Dan W. Roberts's camp. The images were first published in Lou Roberts's book, *A Woman's Reminiscences of Six Years with the Texas Rangers*, published in 1928. Shown is Roberts's headquarters in 1878, with Lou Roberts to the left of the tent opening. Roberts (left) and his sergeant Lamar P. Sieker are by the hack, which was used as an ambulance. (Western History Collections.)

Captain D. W. Roberts' Ranger Camp, below Ft. McKavett, Texas, in Menard county, 1878. Photo made by M. C. Ragsdale.

In 1878, Company D's camp was near Fort McKavett on the San Saba River. Ragsdale caught this scene showing their tents and a figure in the foreground—perhaps the camp cook—who appears to be wearing an apron. Lou Conway and Roberts were married September 13, 1875, in Columbus, Texas. She wrote, "I was much in love with my gallant captain . . . thrilled with the idea of going to the frontier." (Courtesy Western History Collections.)

Captain D. W. Roberts' Ranger Camp, below Ft. McKavett, Texas, in Menard county, 1878.   Photo made by M. C. Ragsdale.

"Dinner in Camp" is how Lou Roberts captioned this image. In camp, the meals were substantial, with no apparent absence of functional cooking utensils. This was not so for the Rangers when on a long scout, which could last for days with only provisions that could be carried in saddlebags or on a pack mule. Note that all of the Rangers retain their pistols, even while dining. (Western History Collections.)

Captain D. W. Roberts' Ranger Camp, below Ft. McKavett, Texas, in Menard county, 1878.   Photo made by M. C. Ragsdale.

All was not excitement in a Ranger camp, as evidenced by this image, "Waiting for Orders," as captioned by Lou Roberts. Ragsdale took this picture of Capt. Roberts's Ranger camp in 1878 in Menard County, below Fort McKavett. The men are obviously ready to go, and all appear relaxed. The reclining figure on the left appears to be dozing off prior to the call to head out. (Western History Collections.)

84

Captain D. W. Roberts' Ranger Camp, below Ft. McKavett, Texas, in Menard county, 1878. Photo made by M. C. Ragsdale.

The men of Company D have received their orders and are preparing to leave on a scout. They will most likely be trailing a fugitive from justice, as by 1878 the Comanche and Kiowa raiding parties were no longer a threat, even though Fort McKavett was considered on the edge of the frontier. None of these Rangers is identified. (Western History Collections.)

Captain D. W. Roberts' Ranger Camp, below Ft. McKavett, Texas, in Menard county, 1878. Photo made by M. C. Ragsdale.

Whether photographer Ragsdale spent more than a day or so in Captain Roberts's camp is unknown. This image, captioned "Home Again After a Scout" by Lou Roberts, shows the men relaxing and their horses grazing out of the camera's eye. Presumably, the figure wearing a suit standing to the right is Captain Roberts. The Ranger uniform was simple: boots, trousers, shirt, vest, hat, and, of course, pistols. (Western History Collections.)

Ira Aten, son of a preacher and one of three brothers who were Rangers, served with distinction and became a sheriff of two Texas counties, Fort Bend and Castro. He wrote his memoir, *Six and One-Half Years in the Ranger Service*, which was published by J. Marvin Hunter in the popular magazine *Frontier Times*. (Western History Collections.)

Joseph Walter Durbin, best known as "J. Walter," was born on February 7, 1860, in Carroll County, Mississippi. Following his Company D years under Capt. Frank Jones, Durbin was elected sheriff of Frio County on November 8, 1892. He served until November 3, 1896. Durbin also penned his memoirs in a book, *Walter Durbin: Texas Ranger and Sheriff*, which was edited by Ranger historian Robert W. Stephens. (Former Texas Rangers Association.)

Young Ira Aten, prepared for action with two belts of ammunition and pistol at the ready, obviously posed for an unknown photographer. Aten later wrote, "I wanted adventure and the romance that goes with it . . . expecting . . . to rescue some pretty girl from the Indians in a daring attack, or from the bandits who infested the Texas border." That never happened, but he served with distinction for Texas, receiving his honorable discharge on July 6, 1895. (Western History Collection.)

Among the most famous Ranger images is this, showing Capt. Frank Jones and the men of Company D, Frontier Battalion. Pictured from left to right are (seated) Robert Bell, Calvin G. Aten, Captain Jones, J. Walter Durbin, James R. Robinson, and Frank Schmid; (standing) James W. King, Baz L. "Bass" Outlaw, Riley Barton, Charles Fusselman, Will Durbin, Ernest Rogers, Charles Barton, and Walter W. Jones. Five of the men pictured here died violently. Smugglers shot Fusselman

and Captain Jones to death. James W. King was killed in a personal confrontation by a knife. Schmid died from wounds received in the courthouse-square battle in Fort Bend County. Baz L. Outlaw was shot to death in an El Paso brawl after he had killed fellow Ranger Joe McKidrict. This image was made when Company D was stationed near Realitos, Uvalde County, in 1887. (Texas Ranger Hall of Fame and Museum.)

Kirchner rests in El Paso's Concordia Cemetery, where infamous gunfighter John Wesley Hardin is also buried. Many come to see the final resting place of Hardin but rarely visit Kirchner's grave. Reenactors do stop by, however, as is evidenced in this image of Kirchner's headstone, with ladies in period costume in the background perhaps visiting Kirchner's grave. His simple stone reads "Carl Kirchner / Nov. 19, 1867 / Jan. 28, 1911." (Author's collection.)

Ranger historian Robert W. Stephens called Carl Kirchner one of the "truly great Rangers of the Trans-Pecos area in the closing years of the nineteenth century." Kirchner joined Company D on May 18, 1889. He was on Pirate Island when Captain Jones was killed in 1893. Kirchner died on January 28, 1911, after contracting typhoid. He is buried in El Paso's Concordia Cemetery. (Western History Collections.)

Walker Rowland Tully served under Capt. Thomas L. Oglesby in the Special Force from August 31, 1880, through November 30, 1881, primarily in La Salle, Dimmit, and Frio Counties. He then married and raised a family. This formal image shows Walker, his wife, Anna Hester Tully, and their children; Julie is standing to the left of her father, Tom is standing behind his sister Hester, and baby Henry is on his mother's lap. (Henry T. Martin Jr.)

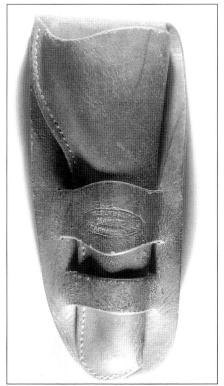

Walker R. Tully farmed and later made leather goods, some of which have become prized collector's items. Here is an example of his work, stamped "W.R. Tully Maker Pearsall, Tex." and a fine holster any Ranger would be proud to wear. This valuable item is still in the family. (Henry T. Martin Jr.)

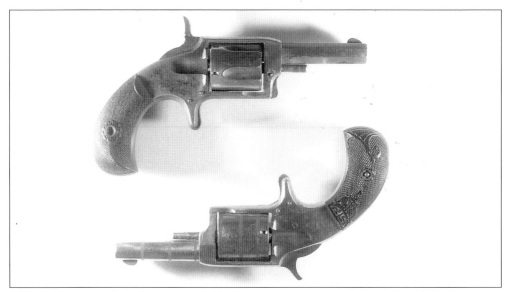

A Texas Ranger rarely had to resort to hideout weapons, as most fighting during the 19th century was done with Sharps rifles or Winchesters. This pair of "pocket pistols" belonged to Walker R. Tully of Captain Oglesby's company. Tully served from August 1, 1880, to February 28, 1881, and was honorably discharged by Captain Oglesby. (Henry T. Martin Jr.)

Walker R. Tully found farming and creating leather goods satisfying after his Ranger service. This damaged image shows Mr. and Mrs. Tully relaxing on the family farm near Pearsall in deep South Texas in the early 1900s. In spite of the damage, the photograph reveals the conditions of life at the end of the 19th century. What may appear to the modern reader as a shack may be the Tully's back porch. (Henry T. Martin Jr.)

"Tell them to meet me—A Texas Ranger" is the message engraved on the headstone of Ranger Oscar F. Pridgen found in Austin's Oakwood Cemetery. Pridgen joined Captain McNelly's Company A on April 1, 1875, and served honorably until August 31, 1875. On his headstone are the dates of his life, June 13, 1854, to June 12, 1944, and this mysterious statement. (Author's collection.)

Daniel W. Roberts remains one of the best-known captains of Company D. Fortunately for history, M.C. Ragsdale photographed Roberts and his troops in 1878. This collage first appeared in Lou Roberts's autobiography. Roberts's image is centered and slightly larger than the others. Shown from left to right are (first row at top) Doug Coalson, Ed Wallace, Lewis Cook, and George Hughes; (second row) Nick Brown, William Sheffield, R.G. Kimbell, Tom Carson, Richard R. Russell, and L.C. Miller; (third row) Ed Sieker, L.P. Sieker, Captain Roberts, Henry Ashburn, and Doctor Gourley; (fourth row): Tom Sparks, Robert Roberts, William Clements, J.L. Rogers, George R. Bingham, and James Renick; (fifth row) James Moore, Sam Henry, E.J. Pound, and Henry Thomas. (Author's collection.)

Five

A RANGER FORCE

Among the most difficult challenges for Governor Coke were the lawlessness and the warring Indian tribes that threatened to push back the frontier line. Coke created the Frontier Battalion to protect settlers and to reduce criminality.

The Frontier Battalion consisted of six companies of 75 men each, with each company commanded by a captain selected by the adjutant general, William Steele. Each captain selected his men. They had to be able to ride and shoot, have a good horse, a weapon, and a willingness to follow orders.

Coke placed veteran John B. Jones with the overall command of the Frontier Battalion. Holding the rank of major, Jones established a high standard for his men. He required them to be of good character, single, and to respect the property of all settlers and honest Texans. Men under indictment or considered drunkards were not accepted.

Due to their success fighting Indians, their purpose soon changed; they worked to reduce all types of criminal activity. They were now lawmen.

In addition to the frequent cases of horse and cattle thieves, bank and train robbers, and lesser crimes, there were many family feuds. Often, these feuds were between families and factions that showed no outward sign of criminality other than the desire to eradicate an enemy for a perceived wrong without resorting to the court system. In Lampasas County, the Horrell-Higgins conflict raged, and in DeWitt and surrounding counties, the Sutton-Taylor feud increased the amount of violence in the area. There was also the "Hoo Doo" war in Mason County. In West Texas, there was the so-called El Paso Salt War.

Among the outlaws who gained notoriety were John Wesley Hardin, Sam Bass, William P. Longley, Brack Cornett, and Will Whitley. Illegal fence cutting created work for the Rangers. As the 19th century waned, new problems arose, such as enforcing quarantine laws, preventing violence at railroad strikes, and taming oil-boom towns. In 1901, the Frontier Battalion ceased to exist except on paper. The new Ranger Force would continue the Frontier Battalion's duties. It was both the beginning of a new century and of a new day for the Texas Rangers.

Capt. Frank Jones, Company D, is shown seated in this rare image made in the late 1880s. The men shown standing in this photograph are, from left to right, Ira Aten, Frank L. Schmid, Charles Fusselman, James R. Robinson, John Woodard "Wood" Saunders, John R. Hughes, Joseph W. Durbin, Bas L. "Bass" Outlaw, James W. Durbin, Ernest Rogers, and Gerry Jones. Five of the men shown died violent deaths. (Author's collection.)

When Captain Jones was killed, he and his squad were on a small island in the middle of the Rio Grande. The marker reads as follows: "Captain Frank Jones / Born in Austin, Texas / 1856 / Killed By Bandits / June 30, 1893 / Near San Elizario / While commanding / Company D / Texas Rangers." Posing with the marker is historian Leon Metz. (Pat Parsons.)

This is a rare image of Company D, Frontier Battalion, in a relaxed pose. This image was made near Ysleta, near the Rio Grande, in 1894. Shown standing is George Tucker. Seated, from left to right, are Thalis T. Cook, US deputy marshal Frank McMahan, Capt. John R. Hughes, William Schmidt, James V. Latham, Carl Kirchner, J.W. Saunders, Joe Sitter, and Ed Palmer. (Joe Sitter and Bob Alexander.)

No doubt the same day this image was made by the same photographer—only more "formally." Pictured seated from left to right are (first row) an unidentified Mexican prisoner, George Tucker, J.W. Saunders, Sgt. Carl Kirchner, and Capt. John R. Hughes; (second row) Frank M. McMahan, William Schmidt, James V. Latham, Joe Sitter, Ed Palmer, and Thalis T. Cook. (Western History Collections.)

Few images of Texas Rangers have been reproduced as often as this iconic image taken at Shafter in Presidio County near the Rio Grande. Why has it become so popular? Not only is it balanced, but it also shows the men proudly displaying their weapons—a popular practice when photographing Rangers during this period. Pictured here, from left to right, are Robert Speaks, Alonzo Van Oden, James Putman, and Capt. John R. Hughes. All show their rifles, giving them the acceptable title of "Winchester Warriors," a term coined by historian Bob Alexander in his recent book of the same title. Of the four men, only Van Oden chose to keep a journal. With numerous clippings and other ephemera, his daughter Ann Jensen published it in 1936, the year of the Texas Centennial. Sadly, both Putman and Hughes ended their own lives, each choosing suicide with a pistol. (John R. Hughes Collection, University of Texas at El Paso.)

Alonzo Van Oden was not the typical Texas Ranger. Historian Robert W. Stephens described him as a man of "rugged, strong countenance" with "intense eyes," who was also "compassionate" and "enjoyed the refinement of the classics, opera and poetry [and] possessed rare intellect and cultural interests." He enlisted in Company D on March 1, 1891, and served continually until May 18, 1894. (John Tanner Jr.)

Alonzo Van Oden was born March 17, 1863. Much is known of the dangers he experienced, thanks to his diary. He counted among his good friends men as different as teetotaler John R. Hughes and the violent alcoholic Baz L. "Bass" Outlaw. Oden died August 11, 1910, in an El Paso hospital. He is buried in the Marfa Cemetery. (James A. Browning Collection.)

Pictured are William A. Scott and his men of Company F. From left to right are (seated) Ed Randall, William Bridwell, Curren Rogers, Allen Newton, and Carlton Hines; (standing) Frank Carmichael, John H. Rogers, Captain Scott, James A. Brooks, Robert Crowder, and James B. Harry. Scott, Brooks, and Rogers were all severely wounded in a gun battle with the Connor gang in Sabine County in 1887. In spite of his wounds, Scott remained in the service until April 30, 1888, most likely retiring at the urging of his new bride. Scott has yet to be the subject of a full biography, although he certainly experienced a great deal of action in his Ranger career. Scott died on November 12, 1913, and is buried in a small Masonic Cemetery near Waelder, Gonzales County. (Texas Ranger Association.)

Calvin Grant Aten

Another one of the Aten brothers who served in Company D was Calvin Grant Aten. Apparently, farmwork did not appeal to him, as he left his father's farm and joined Company D under Frank Jones on April 1, 1888. The tale of his older brother Ira ordering him to put on a six-shooter and be a Ranger may be true—if so, Cal Aten became a worthy addition to the service. In 1889, he was one of the small posse who challenged the Odle brothers in Edwards County. The brothers resisted and were both killed in the ensuing gun battle. Aten resigned from the service on August 31, 1890, at Marfa. He returned to the family home in Round Rock, where he married Mattie Jo Kennedy. The couple moved to the Panhandle, where Aten was employed on the huge XIT Ranch from 1898 to 1904. Aten died April 1, 1939, and is buried in Clarendon. (Betty Aten.)

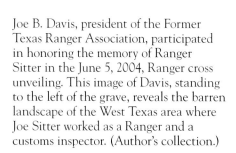

Ranger Joe Sitter of Company D strikes a formal pose in this image made by David P. Barr of San Antonio. Sitter joined Company D on August 1, 1893. He later became a US Customs inspector. Sitter was killed in a gun battle against bandits on May 24, 1915. (Jake Sitter and Bob Alexander.)

Joe B. Davis, president of the Former Texas Ranger Association, participated in honoring the memory of Ranger Sitter in the June 5, 2004, Ranger cross unveiling. This image of Davis, standing to the left of the grave, reveals the barren landscape of the West Texas area where Joe Sitter worked as a Ranger and a customs inspector. (Author's collection.)

William Jesse "Bill" McDonald had an unusual career and is now recognized as one of the "Four Great Captains" along with Brooks, Rogers, and Hughes. His career straddled the closing decade of the 19th century and the beginning decades of the 20th century. In 1891, he was named captain of Company B. While working mainly in the Texas Panhandle, he also traveled down to El Paso to assist other Rangers in preventing a prizefight, dealt with feudists in Colorado County, went down to the southern tip of Texas to investigate the Brownsville troubles in 1906, and also investigated various murder cases in East Texas. His factual life and mythical career have been expertly revealed in *Yours to Command: The Life and Legends of Texas Ranger Captain Bill McDonald* by Harold J. Weiss Jr. (Former Texas Ranger Association.)

Adjutant General W.W. Sterling described McDonald as the "most spectacular Ranger commander of his era." McDonald, according to Sterling, "possessed more showmanship, was given wider publicity, and received better newspaper coverage than Brooks, Rogers, or Hughes." He made good copy, indeed, and lived a long life, dying on January 15, 1918. (Author's collection.)

McDonald impressed the State of Texas sufficiently that a historical marker was placed on his grave in Quanah in 1970. It describes him as a "fearless frontier law officer known for crack marksmanship and lightning-fast disarming of foes." The marker contains several errors but conveys the spirit of the mythical Bill McDonald. (Author's collection.)

No one likes to deal with a strike, but in mid-1894, Rangers were called to Temple to prevent violence and protect the movement of the US mail during the strike. Rangers from Companies F and D were present and posed for this image—appropriately taken before a railroad car—and are, from left to right, (first row) Pvt. Jack Harwell, Pvt. William Schmidt, Pvt. C.B. Fullerton, Pvt. George N. Horton, Pvt. Ed Palmer, Pvt. Joe Nattus, Pvt. James V. Latham, and Pvt. Ed E. Coleman; (second row) Capt. James A. Brooks of Company F, Capt. John R. Hughes of Company D, Pvt. John F. Nix, Col. E.A. Aten, Pvt. Ed F. Connell, Cpl. Thomas M. Ross, Pvt. R.L. Queen, Pvt. A.A. Neely, Pvt. G.J. Cook, and Pvt. Dan Coleman. Their presence prevented violence during the strike. (Western History Collections.)

A group of Texas Rangers from the four battalions and headed by Adjutant General Mabry was called upon to prevent a prizefight that was to take place in Texas in 1896 but actually took place on a sandbar in the Rio Grande while the Rangers watched from the cliffs overlooking the river. The fight was between Bob Fitzsimmons and Peter Maher. These Rangers were photographed by J.C. Burge. Standing side by side in the first row of this photograph are, from to right, Adjutant General W.H. Mabry (in a Napoleonic pose), Capt. John R. Hughes, Capt. James A. Brooks, Capt. William J. McDonald, and Capt. John H. Rogers. (Western History Collections.)

Capt. James A. Brooks and the men of Company A, shown in 1903, appear as heavily armed as their predecessors did in the 1890s. Brooks holds a Mauser "Broom handle" pistol. The company is, from left to right, (first row) Jesse Miller, Sgt. Winfred Bates, Capt. Brooks, and Lonnie Livingston; (second row) Tom Franks, A.Y. Baker, John Puckett, and George Wallis. (Former Texas Ranger Association.)

Rangers were called to Thurber, Erath County, during the coal strike of 1889. Capt. Sam McMurry and Company B responded. Gathered here, from left to right, are John W. Bracken, Arthur Terrell, Tom Malcolm, Tom Platt, Sam Platt, Sterling Price, Tom Hickman, Mollie Platt, W.J.L. Sullivan, Ed Britton, Lon Lewis, John R. Platt, and Phil Best. (Western History Collections.)

At least one other image was made of the McMurry Rangers at Thurber, and with the exception of a missing McMurry, only the relative positions of those photographed changed. Why McMurry is not in this image is unknown, but the scene suggests a pleasant outing. In the first image, Mrs. Platt is holding a Winchester, but now she holds her broom, perhaps ready to sweep away the coal dust. (Western History Collections.)

The Former Texas Rangers Association marks the graves of Texas Rangers with an iron memorial cross. On May 31, 2010, a service was held at the grave of Company E, Frontier Battalion Ranger Lorenzo Hughes. Born on December 31, 1852, he died January 26, 1881. Hughes joined the Rangers on March 13, 1878, and served until August 31, 1880. On retiring, he married Elizabeth Belle Mason, but death claimed him five months later. He is buried in the Bagdad Cemetery near Leander. Shown here is former Ranger James Gant addressing the crowd on the purposes of the Former Texas Ranger Association. The close-up photograph is the cross at Hughes's grave. (Both, Pat Parsons.)

Karnes County sheriff W.T. Morris attempted to arrest suspected horse thief Gregorio Cortez on June 12, 1901. Gunfire erupted, leaving Morris dead and a brother of Cortez dying. Days later, while Cortez was resisting arrest, he killed Gonzales County sheriff Richard M. Glover and deputy Henry Schnabel. After a massive manhunt, Ranger John H. Rogers captured an exhausted Cortez. Included in this photograph, seated from left to right, are Rogers, prisoner Gregorio Cortez, and tracker Manuel Tom with his rifle. (Western History Collections.)

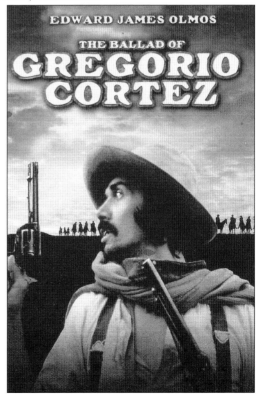

Gregorio Cortez may have started out as only an accused horse thief, but he became a wanted fugitive and the target of one of the largest manhunts in Texas history. He became a celebrity, a legend in his own lifetime. Hollywood later produced a very successful motion picture for television, *The Ballad of Gregorio Cortez,* starring Edward James Olmos. (Bill O'Neal Collection.)

This image shows Rangers as they typically posed in late-19th-century photographs— displaying their weaponry. Shown is Company F in 1882, and the Rangers pictured are, from left to right, (first row) Washington W. Shely, Tom Mabry, Robert Crowder, and Cecilio Charo; (second row) James M. Buck, S.V. "Pete" Edwards, Capt. Joe Shely, George W. Farrow, William T. "Brack" Morris, and Charles Norris. (Former Texas Ranger Association.)

Six

INTO THE 21ST CENTURY

1901

The Ranger Force in 1901 consisted of four companies, each with a captain, one sergeant, and 20 privates. They were empowered to make arrests and serve court papers. The Ranger Force chased robbers and thieves, pursued fugitives from justice, kept order at controversial elections, and enforced antigambling laws and local-option liquor ordinances.

As in the previous century, the Rangers had to deal with border problems. Dissatisfaction increased among Mexican citizens under the government of Pres. Porfirio Diaz. His regime was overthrown by Francisco Madero, but counterrevolutionary activities continued. Rangers had to patrol the border towns to prevent revolutionary plots from being formed on US soil. Smuggling guns and other weapons, as well as human trafficking, demanded constant surveillance. Often, there were clashes between Rangers and criminals, with death on both sides the result.

Elsewhere in the state, there were racial problems between whites and blacks as well as whites and Mexicans. Threats of lynch mobs were frequent. Labor disputes, strikes, and personal feuds demanded the presence of Rangers as well as local law officials.

On May 8, 1935, the Texas Rangers became part of the department of public safety (DPS), which remains true today. Ranger headquarters in Austin became the center of a professional training program. There would be constant communication with the highway patrol, county and city officers, other state agencies, and the federal government. The Ranger Force now became, officially and for the first time, the Texas Rangers.

The three-century-long history of the Texas Rangers is a glorious history, indeed. The Rangers' storied past is preserved in private collections as well as in the Texas State Archives in Austin and the Texas Ranger Hall of Fame and Museum in Waco. Inside the museum's walls is the largest collection of artifacts relating to Ranger history in the world. There is also a gift shop where visitors can purchase books, hats, cards, and a host of other collectible items, as well as a splendid research center and non-circulating library.

Dominated by the Knights of Labor, labor organizations grew in the 1880s. Jay Gould's southwest railroad's 3,300 employees struck from March to May 1886, causing repercussions over the state. Rangers were called in to protect property and prevent violence in Fort Worth, union headquarters. This image shows Capt. George W. Schmitt and Company C at Fort Worth in 1886. Rangers present for this photograph are, from left to right, J.W. Owens, Henry Putts, James C. Barringer, Sam R. Pickett, Charles Kuhly, George W. Clark, James R. Robinson, J. Walter Durbin, Albert C. Grimes, and Captain Schmitt. (Former Texas Rangers Association.)

This unusual image shows Ranger R.A. "Bob" Crowder on a motorcycle, with John Lowery, leading a centennial parade in Wichita Falls in 1936. Note the rifle in his "saddle" boot. (Former Texas Ranger Association.)

This is an unusual image of Texas Rangers, as in most pictures they proudly displayed their weaponry, and here their weapons are concealed. In another break with tradition, they are wearing no boots. Oscar J. Rountree, an Arizona Ranger from 1903 to 1906 and a Texas Ranger from 1907 to 1910, is shown on the left. In the center is Capt. Frank Johnson, who was elected sheriff of Mitchell County in 1902 but resigned in July 1907. On the right is Jesse C. Sanders, son of Capt. J.J. Sanders. Johnson and Sanders died natural deaths, but Rountree was killed in a San Antonio saloon on August 19, 1910. (Western History Collections.)

John R. Hughes became an iconic figure after his forced resignation in January 1915. Enjoying life to the fullest, he traveled throughout much of the Southwest, visiting friends and old Ranger companions. This image, originally a photograph by L.A. Wilke, was turned into a colored postcard in 1939, when Hughes was 84 years old. (Author's collection.)

At the Wild West History Association (WWHA) Roundup in San Antonio in 2009, a panel shared its knowledge of Ranger history. Those gathered to share their expertise are, from left to right, Paul N. Spellman, author of biographies of Captain Rogers and Captain Brooks; Chuck Parsons, author of a biography of Capt. John R. Hughes; moderator Bob Alexander, author of *Winchester Warriors: Texas Rangers of Company D, 1874–1901*; and Rick Miller, whose biography of Maj. John B. Jones is forthcoming. (Bob Alexander.)

Among the many special guests at the WWHA Roundup in 2009 was Ranger Joaquin Jackson (right), shown here with author Bob Alexander. Jackson served from April 1, 1966, until his retirement on October 1, 1993. His autobiography, *One Ranger: A Memoir*, remains one of the top-selling books from the University of Texas Press. Jackson now heads a private investigation firm based in Alpine. (Daniel Patterson.)

At the 2009 WWHA meeting, historian Bob Alexander and his publisher presented copies of Alexander's history of Company D to each member of the company. Shown is WWHA president Robert G. McCubbin (left), who presented a plaque to Capt. Hank Whitman Jr. to honor the work of the Rangers. Whitman is now deputy assistant director of the Texas Rangers. (Daniel Patterson.)

Bob Alexander's book *Winchester Warriors* was released by the University of North Texas (UNT) Press prior to the WWHA Roundup in 2009. Shown is UNT press director Ron Chrisman announcing the book, which covers the enlisted man's life during the frontier period. This was the first time a Ranger company received a book detailing the history of the Rangers' earlier years. (Daniel Patterson.)

The Texas Ranger Hall of Fame and Museum in Waco "commemorates the service and sacrificing of 30 Texas Rangers who gave their lives in the line of duty or made significant contributions to the development of the service." The list ranges from Stephen F. Austin and William Wallace to Robert A. Crowder and Manuel T. Gonzaullas. Shown is an exterior view of the museum. (Pat Parsons.)

Tools of the modern Texas Rangers shown here are only the most obvious. The pistol, the badge, and the gun belt are natural necessities for a Ranger. The current Ranger will feel as comfortable on a horse as in an automobile or a helicopter, or on a motorcycle. He is also a detective and in general an expert with all types of crime. (Former Texas Rangers Association.)

Homer Garrison Jr. transformed the "old" Texas Rangers into the new and highly effective modern Rangers. In 1938, Garrison became director of the DPS and chief of the Texas Rangers. He developed more effective programs for crime patrol, police traffic supervision, driver licensing, vehicle inspection, defense and disaster service, and police training. (Former Texas Rangers Association.)

Colonel Garrison never avoided an opportunity to encourage young people to have respect for the law and to know the importance of being aware of their surroundings for safety's sake. Here, he is shown with an unidentified youngster, who appears to have plans to someday become a Texas Ranger. (Former Texas Rangers Association.)

Garrison was well aware of the importance of image and the use of the media. In 1945, Brooks County selected July 2 as "Texas Ranger Day." Audie Murphy (right), the most decorated soldier of World War II, had always wanted to become a Texas Ranger. He was chosen to lead the parade. Garrison and Murphy are shown here on that very special day for Brooks County. (Former Texas Ranger Association.)

Another noted 20th-century Texas Ranger was Manuel T. "Lone Wolf" Gonzaullas (left). He also attended the celebration in Brooks County and is shown here with honorary Texas Ranger Audie Murphy. The Spanish-born Ranger developed a distinguished record as a lawman. He preferred to work alone. "I went into a lot of fights by myself, and I came out by myself, too," he noted. He was nicknamed "El Lobo Solo" (the lone wolf) by bandits. (Former Texas Ranger Association.)

Ranger C.L. "Blackie" Blackwell appears ready for war while serving at Presidio in 1921. He rose to the rank of sergeant while serving under Capt. Jerry Gray. Blackwell's mode of dress is more similar to Ranger dress of the 19th century than the 20th. (Former Texas Rangers Association.)

Among the many notorious criminals of the 20th century, none perhaps caused more terror among citizens and work for all types of law enforcement officers than the crime spree of Henry Lee Lucas (far right). He boasted of many murders. Here, Ranger Phil Ryan (third from left) is shown with unidentified officers of Montague County examining the grave of a person who might be one of Lucas's victims. (Former Texas Rangers Association.)

A special year in Texas history was 1936, when it celebrated its centennial. A significant celebration was held in Dallas, and the organizers were very aware of the importance of Texas Rangers in the state's history. The DPS provided a special building for all Rangers, active and retired, and placed the words "Texas Rangers" prominently for all to see. This is only one of many images made at the time, but unfortunately, only a few men have been identified. Included in this photograph are (first row, eighth from right) the iconic John R. Hughes, 81 years old, with a distinguished white beard; (first row, seventh from right) Capt. W.L. Wright, who served a total of 20 years as a Ranger; (second row, third from left); and Tolbert F. McKinney, in a dark necktie, who served as a Ranger under Hughes. (Former Texas Ranger Association.)

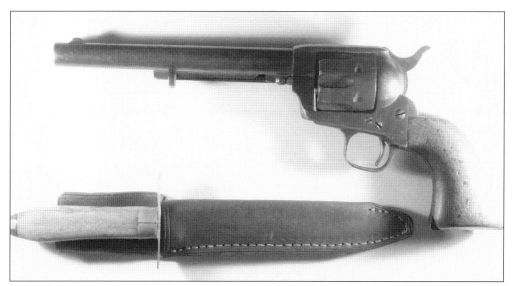

The old-time Rangers pictured in 1936 on the preceding page hold canes to help them deal with the infirmities of age. In their younger days, they carried such weapons as a Colt revolver and a Bowie knife. These items belonged to Ranger Walker R. Tully and today are prized possessions of his descendants. The serial number of the Colt is 27877, and it was manufactured in 1876. The scabbard was made by Tully himself. (Henry T. Martin Jr.)

On April 30, 1961, the *Texas Ranger of 1960* statue was dedicated in the lobby of Love Field in Dallas. Jay Banks was the model, and the legendary but mythical "One Riot, One Ranger" was engraved on the statue's base. Regrettably, few travelers are aware of the actual history of the Texas Rangers. (Bill O'Neal Collection.)

One of the greatest living historians remains Robert M. Utley, former chief historian of the National Park Service, a founding member and president of the Western History Association, and the author of more than a dozen books on the American West. His two-volume study *Lone Star Justice* and *Lone Star Lawmen* will remain classic studies. (Oxford University Press.)

A historian equally important to Texas history is Stephen L. Hardin, shown here speaking at the 2009 WWHA Roundup. Among Hardin's early books was *Texas Rangers*. His latest works include two authoritative studies—*Texan Iliad: A Military History of the Texas Revolution* and *Texian Macabre: The Melancholy Tale of a Hanging in Early Houston*. (Daniel Patterson.)

Zane Grey's Westerns are perhaps most engrossing when they depict a hero with internal conflicts—often an innocent man turned outlaw due to forces beyond his control. A moral dilemma drives the story of *Lone Star Ranger*, wherein Buck Duane is forced to kill and becomes a Ranger with the knowledge that he is hunted both by lawmen and outlaws. Grey dedicated this novel, published in 1915, to Captain Hughes and his Texas Rangers. (Bill O'Neal Collection.)

Photographs of John R. Hughes as a young Ranger are rare. After his retirement, however, he seemed to attract photographers, as there are numerous later images of him. Shown here is the old Ranger captain in an image perhaps dating from the year of the Texas centennial, when he was a special guest of the state fair committee in Dallas. (Former Texas Ranger Association.)

Clayton Moore
Lone Ranger

Thanks to radio and television and the motion picture industry, the fabled Lone Ranger and his faithful friend Tonto have become recognized film icons the world over. In spite of their popularity, the Lone Ranger and Tonto were totally fictitious. The idea of a lawman wearing a mask, riding a white stallion, and leaving silver bullets to remember him by appealed to thousands of youngsters. (Bill O'Neal Collection.)

Hollywood released the motion picture *Bonnie and Clyde* on August 13, 1967, starring Faye Dunaway and Warren Beatty as the romanticized bank robbers and killers. The movie was a tremendous hit at the box office. Although having easy access to accurate accounts, film writers blundered in having Ranger Frank Hamer (Denver Pyle) captured, tied to a tree, and then kissed by Bonnie. In truth, Hamer had resigned from the Rangers when he began his pursuit of Bonnie and Clyde, was never captured by the pair, and never saw them until the day he and his posse killed them. In 1968, Hamer's widow and son brought suit against the motion picture for defamation of Hamer's character and won an undisclosed amount. Shown on this page are the real Frank Hamer as a young Ranger and the above-mentioned scene from the motion picture. (Both, Bill O'Neal Collection.)

The legendary John Wayne starred in many Westerns, but in only three did he play the role of a Texas Ranger or a character who fought against a Ranger. He played Ethan Edwards in *The Searchers* (1936), directed by John Ford and considered by many to be one of the greatest Westerns ever made. In *The Comancheros* (1961), Wayne was fictional Ranger captain Jake Cutter. (Bill O'Neal Collection.)

Among the most successful motion pictures based on fictional Texas Rangers, few were as popular as *Lonesome Dove*—not only because of the outstanding actors but also because of the gripping story line, which is based on the novel of the same title by Larry McMurtry. Robert Duval played an old grizzled former Ranger named Gus McCrae, while Tommy Lee Jones played Woodrow Call. The made-for-television Western was a blockbuster and remains popular today. Students of Ranger history may recognize some actual incidents that are re-created on the screen. (Bill O'Neal Collection.)

FURTHER READING

The following is a list of recommended reading about the Texas Rangers. It is only a sampling of the many works about this popular subject.

Alexander, Bob. *Winchester Warriors: Texas Rangers of Company D, 1874–1901.* Denton, TX: University of North Texas Press, 2009.

Cox, Mike. *The Texas Rangers: Wearing the Cinco Peso, 1821–1900.* New York: Forge Books, 2008.

———. *The Texas Rangers: Time of the Ranger: From 1900 to the Present.* New York: Forge Books, 2009.

Harris, Charles H., III, Frances Harris, and Louis R. Sadler. *Texas Ranger Biographies: Those Who Served, 1910–1921.* Albuquerque: University of New Mexico Press, 2009.

——— and Louis R. Sadler. *The Texas Rangers and the Mexican Revolution, 1910–1920.* Albuquerque: University of New Mexico Press, 2004.

Jackson, Joaquin, and David Wilkinson. *One Ranger: A Memoir.* Austin: University of Texas Press, 2005.

——— and James L. Haley. *One Ranger Returns.* Austin: University of Texas Press, 2008.

Moore, Stephen L. *Savage Frontier: Rangers, Riflemen, and Indian Wars in Texas*, Vols. I–IV. Denton, TX: University of North Texas Press, 2002, 2006, 2007, and 2010.

O'Neal, Bill. *Reel Rangers: Texas Rangers in Movies, TV, Radio & Other Forms of Popular Culture.* Austin: Eakin Press, 2008.

Parsons, Chuck. *Captain L.H. McNelly: Texas Ranger.* Austin: State House Press, 2001.

———. *John B. Armstrong: Texas Ranger and Pioneer Rancher.* College Station, TX: Texas A&M University Press, 2007.

——— and Donaly E. Brice. *Texas Ranger N.O. Reynolds: The Intrepid.* Honolulu: Talei Publishers, Inc., 2005.

Spellman, Paul N. *Captain John H. Rogers, Texas Ranger.* Denton, TX: University of North Texas Press, 2003.

———. *Captain J.A. Brooks, Texas Ranger.* Denton, TX: University of North Texas Press, 2007.

Utley, Robert M. *Lone Star Justice: The First Century of the Texas Rangers.* New York: Oxford University Press, 2002.

———. *Lone Star Lawmen: The Second Century of the Texas Rangers.* New York: Oxford University Press, 2007.

Weiss, Harold J., Jr. *Yours to Command: The Life and Legend of Texas Ranger Captain Bill McDonald.* Denton, TX: University of North Texas Press, 2009.

Wilkins, Frederick. *The Law Comes to Texas: The Texas Rangers, 1870–1901.* Austin: State House Press, 1999.

DISCOVER THOUSANDS OF LOCAL HISTORY BOOKS FEATURING MILLIONS OF VINTAGE IMAGES

Arcadia Publishing, the leading local history publisher in the United States, is committed to making history accessible and meaningful through publishing books that celebrate and preserve the heritage of America's people and places.

Find more books like this at
www.arcadiapublishing.com

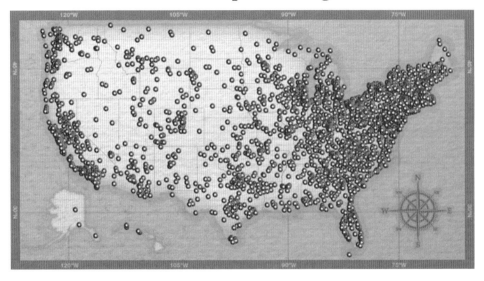

Search for your hometown history, your old stomping grounds, and even your favorite sports team.